ALTERNATE ROOTS

RACE, RHETORIC, AND MEDIA SERIES
Davis W. Houck, *General Editor*

ALTERNATE ROOTS

Ethnicity, Race, and Identity in Genealogy Media

CHRISTINE SCODARI

UNIVERSITY PRESS OF MISSISSIPPI / JACKSON

Research for and publication of this book has been generously supported by
Florida Atlantic University®, the Florida Atlantic University Foundation, the
Dorothy F. Schmidt College of Arts and Letters, and the Morrow Fund.

www.upress.state.ms.us

Designed by Peter D. Halverson

The University Press of Mississippi is a member of the
Association of University Presses.

First printing 2018

∞

Library of Congress Cataloging-in-Publication Data

Names: Scodari, Christine, author.
Title: Alternate roots : ethnicity, race, and identity in genealogy media /
Christine Scodari.
Description: Jackson : University Press of Mississippi, [2018] | Series:
Race, rhetoric, and media series | Includes bibliographical references and
index. |
Identifiers: LCCN 2017058298 (print) | LCCN 2018000590 (ebook) | ISBN
9781496817792 (epub single) | ISBN 9781496817808 (epub institutional) |
ISBN 9781496817815 (pdf single) | ISBN 9781496817822 (pdf institutional)
| ISBN 9781496817785 (hardcover : alk. paper)
Subjects: LCSH: Identity (Psychology)—Genealogy. | Genealogy—Social aspects.
Classification: LCC CS14 (ebook) | LCC CS14 .S36 2018 (print) | DDC
929.1—dc23
LC record available at https://lccn.loc.gov/2017058298

British Library Cataloging-in-Publication Data available

CONTENTS

ACKNOWLEDGMENTS

Without the data, photos, diaries, letters, narratives, family trees, documents, and other mementos fleshing out this examination of the institutions, texts, technologies, and practices of family history, *Alternate Roots* could not have come to fruition. Sincere appreciation goes to online and in-person archives and the told and untold family members from two continents, both living and deceased, who safeguarded and passed on information and artifacts, in many instances never knowing they would find their way to me. They include, among others, Walter Arlia, Bob Barone, Edie Barone, Kate Barone, Audrey Buglione, Elisabetta Campanella, Mary Cafazzo, Louise Carpenter, Mike Crivello, Susan Derrick, Barbara Dickson, Christina Ervolino, Harry Foglietta, Shirley Garrison, Nicole Jones, Belinda Micciulli Martin, Angela Micciulli, Attilio Micciulli, Carmelo Micciulli, David Micciulli, Edward Micciulli, Francesco Micciulli, Massimo Micciulli, Paolo Micciulli, Rita Micciulli, Charles Scodari, Dominick Scodari, Frank Scodari, Genevieve Scodari, Marion Scodari, Nicholas Scodari, Francesco Scuteri, Nicola Scuteri, Mary Sheridan, Gerard Simonette, Frances Taylor, Sal Vitale, and Evelyn Zampino.

ALTERNATE ROOTS

INTRODUCTION

Genealogy Today

The true picture of the past flits by. The past can be seized only as an
image that flashes up when it can be recognized and is never seen
again. . . . For every image of the past that is not recognized by the
present as one of its own concerns threatens to disappear irretrievably.

—WALTER BENJAMIN, "THESES ON THE PHILOSOPHY OF HISTORY"

JOURNEYING INTO FAMILY HISTORY

Beyond the occasional query when I was a child, my interest in something
called family history began in the early 1980s, not long after a reunion—or
more precisely, a *reconciliation*—brought together the Italian and American
branches of my mother's paternal-line family. In addition to grandparents,
parents, siblings, aunts, uncles, and cousins along this lineage, the American
branch included my mother's nieces, nephews, and in-laws, some of whom
were/are also genetically related to my father because of three marriages
between the two families.

If not for the politics of class, which, in the context of southern Italian
identity was intimately connected to race and ethnicity, there might never
have been a need for reconciliation. My mother's patrilineal great-grandfather, a landowner and doctor, had disinherited his eldest son, her immigrant
grandfather, when he married a woman from a family of *contadini* (peasant
farmers) who worked on his land in the southern region of Calabria, where
elevated class status stood as a bulwark against racially tinged prejudice
emanating from the north. But one of my mother's aunts wanted to reconcile
with her Italian family before she died, and her wish was fulfilled.

Interest piqued again when my father took early retirement from the
federal government and had lots of time on his hands. Our family home was

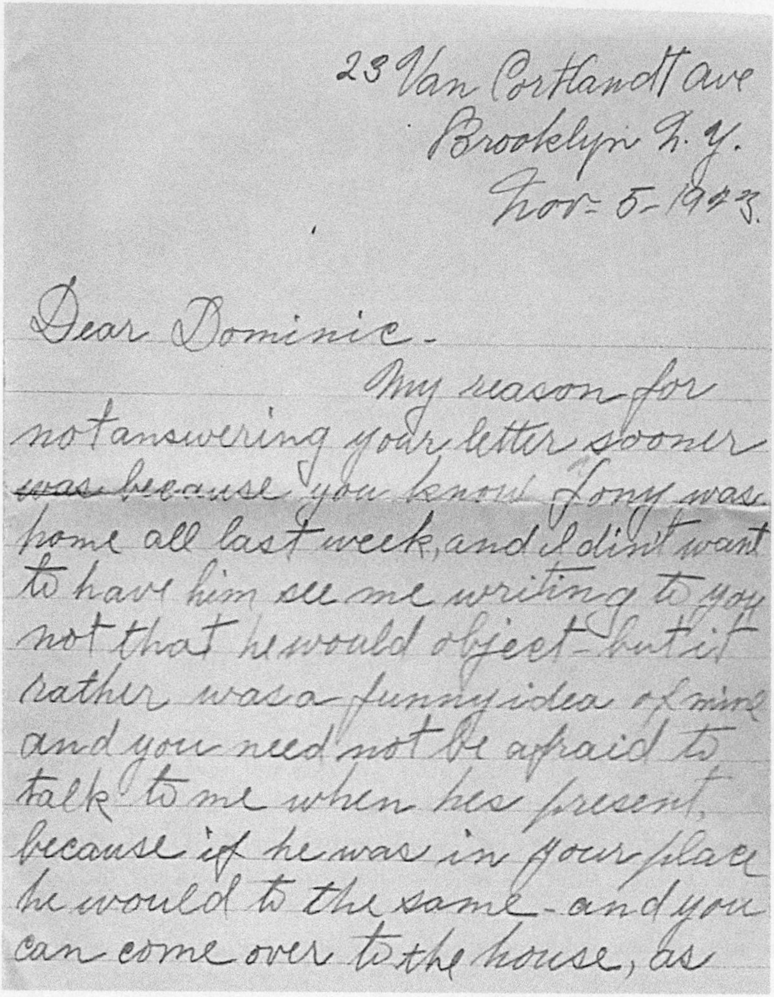

23 Van Cortlandt ave
Brooklyn N. Y.
Nov= 5-1923.

Dear Dominic-
My reason for
not answering your letter sooner
was because you know Tony was
home all last week, and I dint want
to have him see me writing to you
not that he would object-but it
rather was a funny idea of mine
and you need not be afraid to
talk to me when hes present,
because if he was in your place
he would to the same-and you
can come over to the house, as

Figure 1.1: 1923 courtship letter from my grandmother to my grandfather.

located in the suburbs of Washington, DC, providing him with easy access to the National Archives, where he obtained copies of the 1900 census and naturalization certificates relating to his paternal lineage. Somewhat later, my father's little sister, who was more like a big sister to me, gave me some family mementos. A linen-covered box of letters exchanged by her parents when they were courting in the 1920s was particularly intriguing. In one 1923 letter (figure 1.1), the seventeen-year-old girl who would become my grandmother commiserates with the young man who would become my grandfather about her older brother's disapproval of their relationship. The brother was apparently having relationship issues of his own. My grandparents-to-be were communicating by mail even though they both lived in Brooklyn, proving once again that forms of social media interaction existed long before the digital age. I later discovered that at age six, my future grandmother had arrived by ship on American shores just as the *Titanic*, operated by the same shipping line, met its tragic end.

In the early 1990s, I acquired rudimentary software, information, photos, and documents and cobbled together a five-generation family tree to transcribe into an old-media family history album for my parents. As a baby boomer, I was among those later discussed in news reports of genealogy's new popularity who were engaging in the hobby with the help of digital media (see Wee; Shute). I believe, however, that the journey into family history is often about *any* generation navigating middle age, caring for elders in decline, and coming to terms with the inevitable. Like many cultural practices associated with people in their middle or senior years, genealogy has been woefully understudied, especially in terms of marginal identities.

In 2003, my mother suffered the first of a series of strokes that eventually took her to a nursing home. Only a few years later, my father began displaying signs of what we later learned was Alzheimer's disease. In addition to many other things, memory was at stake.

In 2010, I took family leave from my job to help oversee my parents' care and refocused on genealogy, this time using Internet archives, commercial websites, and newer software designed for integration with online databases. My father's little sister had died in 2009, bequeathing to me additional family artifacts. After I determined that many cultural texts and practices of family history warranted critical academic analysis and that I could simultaneously engage in family history and partially fulfill my role as a scholar, I became even more engrossed in the activity. I set about learning a language that I had mostly heard as a child when adults felt a need to swear in the presence of tender ears. I read up on Italian and Italian American history, consulted with close and distant family via old and new media, ordered microfilm of Italian records, and watched family history television.

My explorations of Italian American history deepened my sense of ethnic identity as well as my empathy for and understanding of those who have experienced ethnically and/or racially based or inflected struggles that in many cases have been exceedingly brutal and unrelenting. In these terms, my racial privilege in the here and now became even clearer. I learned more about the 1891 lynching of eleven Sicilians in New Orleans as described in the 2015 PBS documentary series *The Italian Americans*. I also probed the suppression of Italian language and culture during World War II, which contributed to the subsequent decline of spoken Italian in the United States (see DiStasi). My father and I had our DNA tested for genetic ancestry. Although I quickly confirmed that many scholars dismiss genealogy as a self-involved, elitist practice, I tested myself to reenvision it as a critical pursuit in my interrogation of relevant institutions of production, technologies, texts, audience readings, and participatory practices bound up in the media and culture of family history.

ISSUES AND TRAJECTORIES

On 6 June 2015, the first Global Family Reunion, founded by author/journalist A. J. Jacobs, convened in New York City with the goal of highlighting the interrelatedness of the wider human family, in part through establishment of a *global* family tree linking trees posted on various websites. For the previous two decades, the media had noted the increasing numbers of individuals fashioning family trees prompted by, among other things, the aging of baby boomers, a "sense of mortality" (Wee A1), a "proliferation of Internet genealogy sites," and a "growing pride in ethnicity" (Shute 76). According to Eric Wee's 1997 assessment in the *Washington Post*, not since TV's airing of *Roots* twenty years earlier had the hobby been so popular. A spate of new genealogy-themed television series and Internet-driven genetic ancestry testing services capitalizing on the 2003 mapping of the human genome have now emerged. These developments present new and pressing issues for critical analysis, particularly along the lines of race and ethnicity.

Some observers critique genealogy as a limiting, "navel-gazing" (Kramer "Mediatizing" 442) pursuit devoted to, as philosopher Martin Saar cautions, "your own culture, your milieu, your family, your genus" (236). Also implying that criticism is not the amateur genealogist's first order of business, communication scholar Ronald Bishop found accuracy to be the central concern among his family historian survey subjects. One of them declared, "I just love to read and know more about my ancestors and I don't care what it is just so I can properly document it" ("Grand Scheme" 405).

Other observers emphasize that family historians seek to connect their forebears to historical events. For instance, sociologist Anne-Marie Kramer asserts that "genealogy allows people to personalise the past" (qtd. in Amot). Similarly, Neil Silberman and Margaret Purser, writing in the field of heritage studies, argue that genealogy has been transformed from a "passively acquired record of a pedigree to reinforce elite social status or inheritance" into a "process" and "facilitator of reconnection—in this case, to history" (locations 851–56). François Weil's *Family Trees*, an American history of genealogy, acknowledges that it has been practiced not only as a "goal in itself" or as a "means for economic, moral, or religious results or benefits" but also as a way to establish "individual and collective identities" (locations 68–74).

These predispositions might still preclude a *critical* posture—an ability to individuate and empathize with people otherwise perceived only as statistics or abstractions and cultivate compassion and action in response to *their* oppositional struggles. Consequently, making the leap from individual to collective identity is only one leg of this journey toward a critical genealogy; recognizing affinities between one's own collectives and those of others, often separated by time, space, race, ethnicity, class, and/or gender may be more illuminating and demanding. Acknowledging certain affinities while observing distinctions related to specific identities and contexts is harder yet.

In suggesting that one cannot fully appreciate an individual genealogy without positioning it within a constellation of families, peoples, eras, and events, the Global Family Reunion seeks to stimulate such critical possibilities. In one aspect, it envisions genealogy as family history, which goes beyond the mere construction of a pedigree (see Guelke and Timothy 1–2). Scholars also gesture in this direction. Saar contends that genealogy has its greatest critical impact "when it turns to objects whose meaning and validity is affected by revealing their historicity" (233). Similarly, Christine Sleeter suggests that white educators investigate their family histories to perform a "critical analysis of their own lives, examining themselves as culturally and historically located beings" (121). From the perspectives of journalism and memory studies, Barbie Zelizer acknowledges that *collective* memory goes beyond the personal to the circulation of memories and histories given meaning by a group before potentially attaining universality. Anthropologists Angela Labrador and Elizabeth Chilton attest that genealogy is not only "individualized . . . but immersed in the social concepts of geography, demography, citizenship, ethnicity, tourism, and diasporic movements" and thus "can be elitist and exclusionary, and/or democratic and inclusionary" (5–6). Film studies scholar Annette Kuhn argues that family reminiscences and artifacts encourage the exploration of "connections between 'public' historical events, structures of feeling, family dramas, relations of class, national identity and gender, and 'personal' memory" (5). And in "Genealogical

Identities," geographer Catherine Nash concurs that genealogy offers an expansive sense of identity that can lead one to consider the plight of others.

Consequently, despite the possible pitfalls, engaging in or with genealogy media and culture can unearth various histories of oppression, domination, resistance, flight, and dispersal and provide recognition of associations with and distinctions from ongoing struggles. However, deliberate interventions or unanticipated insights must occur to rupture and liberate otherwise hemmed-in public displays and/or practices of heritage.

As my parents' faltering memories prompted me to revisit the genealogical project I adopted from my father years earlier, I immersed myself in genealogy culture. As a consequence of the degree of cultural competency I possess as a professor of critical media and cultural studies, I endeavored to maintain a self-reflexive, autoethnographic relationship to genealogy's texts and practices and consciously privileged critical perspectives based in race/ethnicity, class, gender, and nation, among others. Although *genealogy* appears in the title of this volume, which often uses that term interchangeably with *family history*, a critical perspective necessarily grows out of the broader endeavor of family history, which utilizes interpersonal information and family narratives and goes beyond the direct ancestral line.

However, one might ask whether such a critical approach can be translated to a wider swath of genealogy practitioners. Venturing beyond the nuts and bolts of genealogical practice, my analysis widens the scope to include an assortment of relevant critical objects as it answers an overarching question: To what extent do media texts, practices, institutions, tools, and technologies of family history mobilize critical postures and objectives regarding race and ethnicity, and how might those objectives be rendered more complicit with such an orientation? In grappling with this broad-ranging query, subsidiary issues arise. First, it is crucial to determine whether the components of family history culture produce, in terms of race and ethnicity, critical negotiations of individual identity, connections between the individual and the collective historical, and/or telling links between historical and contemporary struggles.

The second and third questions follow from this starting point: Do family history practices, institutions, representations, and participatory cultures resistively probe racial and ethnic identity in terms of hybridity and/or intersectionality and/or hegemonically reproduce postracial and other *post*-orientations in which racist, nativist, or other exclusionary perspectives go unrecognized? Focusing on the *hybridity* of identities—what cultural studies theorist Stuart Hall refers to as their "ruptures and discontinuities" ("Cultural Identity" 225)—is vital in evaluating representations and interpretations of history and identity in genealogy cultures. Hall maintains that one should not characterize diasporic identities "by essence or purity, but . . . by a conception of 'identity' which lives with and through, not despite, difference; by *hybridity*" (235). Communication scholar Catherine Squires pronounces hybridity to be the "liminal space where negotiation and struggle occur," but cautions that while "hybridity offers potential to subvert dominant narratives of purity . . . these opportunities are neither guaranteed nor the only possibilities that may emerge" (211). Sociologist Katharine Tyler's ethnographic research highlights genealogy's role in establishing mixed-race identity, which, she argues, enables opposition to "the essentialist folk conception of racial difference" (476). Acknowledging hybrid identity as part of the process, geographer Dallen Timothy discerns that those family history practitioners who are the "more visible targets of racism and bigotry" can benefit from family history tourism, which aids in the negotiation of "diasporic identities" (129). Conversely, media scholar Angharad Valdivia warns that "we need to explore the gains and losses incurred in cultural and population mixtures rather than acritically celebrate mixture, as commodity culture urges us to do" (locations 1296–1302).

Moreover, in theorizing hybridity through a prism of *intersectionality*—that is, the recognition of manifestations of oppression that arise when two or more aspects of identity are taken together—sociologist Patricia Hill Collins argues that the impact of having multiple, marginal identities is not simply additive:

> Intersectionality refers to particular forms of intersecting oppressions, for example, intersections of race and gender, or of sexuality and nation. Intersectional paradigms remind us that oppression cannot be reduced to one fundamental type, and that oppressions work together in producing injustice. (Black 21)

In her article on intersections of identity as they operate within the family construct, Collins clarifies: "As opposed to examining gender, race, class, and nation, as separate systems of oppression, intersectionality explores how these systems mutually construct one another" ("All in the Family" 63). She argues that it is within the presumably "natural" family that people first position themselves within hierarchical arrangements relating to race, gender, ethnicity, class, and sexuality and understand them as similarly "natural." For example, a familial knowledge that renders children subordinate to their parents and women subordinate to their ostensibly more mature husbands is echoed in a societal belief that nonwhites are "intellectually underdeveloped" (65). In such a way, hierarchies are internalized as "natural" and inevitable. Racial constructions operating in other times and/or places can likewise be unpacked, Collins argues, as long as race, however conceived, operates as a "principle of social organization" (66).

This volume looks not only at how family historians might understand, in specifically contextual ways, intersections involving race and/or ethnicity that might have formed within families but also at how to decipher their relevance to historical and ongoing relations of power *beyond* the family through engagement in/with the texts and practices of genealogy media and culture. Perspectives related to hybridity and intersectionality gesture toward making connections between and among identities as well as between localized findings and broader contexts and issues that might, given only cursory attention, seem tangential to chronicling a particular family history.

Considering the hegemonic impacts of postidentity discourses grounded in postracial, postfeminist, and/or postclass orientations is also crucial. *Postracism* (or *postracialism*) has variously been referred to as *post–civil rights*, or the notion that the civil rights movement has done its work, creating a "backlash" against its supposed excesses (Springer 253), or as *postrace*, the "continued centrality of race within this ideology where race is ostensibly immaterial" (Joseph 521). *Postfeminism* follows suit. For gender studies analysts Elaine Hall and Marnie Rodriguez, postfeminism's key claim is that feminism has advanced the status of women but no longer applies, since younger women view sexism as individual, not systemic. Yvonne Tasker and Diane Negra, film studies theorists, add that "postfeminist culture . . . works to commodify feminism via the figure of a woman as empowered consumer" (2). Arguing for the pivotal role of class, communication scholar Kathleen Feyh writes that *post-Marxism* "provides ideological support, even radical cover, to neoliberal capitalism" (237). Communication scholar Kent Ono links class with postracism, maintaining that the latter "reproduces the age-old mythology . . . that by pulling oneself up by one's bootstraps, working hard, acting ethically, playing fair, and not asking for help it is possible to achieve the American dream" (229). Whether in terms or race, ethnicity, gender, class, and/or other factors, it is vital to decipher whether genealogy-related representations, such as those contained in the plethora of recent celebrity family history television programs, fixate on transcendent, contemporary figures, implying that the marginality that may have challenged them or their families in the past is no longer operative.

Beyond dissecting genetic ancestry discourses and practices according to whether revelations of hybridity help destabilize the "folk conception of racial difference" (Tyler 476), a fourth question emerges: Do media discourses and related practices specific to genetic ancestry privilege ethnocentricity, patrilineal connections, and genetic rather than cultural notions of kinship and/or provide cover or grist for essentialist, racist, and/or racializing rhetoric? Sociologist Catherine Lee questions genetic genealogy's effect on society's definitions of kinship and issues of immigration. She recounts a case in which DNA testing invalidated an African immigrant's fatherly status, dooming his petition to have his sons join him in the United States. "Genetic analysis does not always provide unwavering answers to how people are related," Lee maintains, "and certainly not to how they understand their attachments to one another" (locations 509–11).

Indeed, in a *Melissa Harris Perry Show* discussion of the 2015 Global Family Reunion that aired on 31 May 2015, Jacobs underscored the goal of having individuals engaging in family history ultimately realize that the concept of family goes beyond genetics. Others on the panel went further. In advocating alternative definitions of family, Perry, a political science professor at Wake Forest University, stated, "If everybody's my cousin, then nobody's my cousin." Writer, radio host, and comic Jamie Kilstein concurred that "self-made" families should not be neglected. Finally, Cristina Beltrán, a social and cultural analyst at New York University, asserted that practitioners should feel a "collective responsibility" when confronting historical linkages to perpetrators of such abominable institutions and events as slavery and the Holocaust.

The racial/ethnic implications of genetic ancestry science are particularly thorny. In their introduction to *Revisiting Race in a Genomic Age*, medical ethicists Barbara A. Koenig, Sandra Soo-Jin Lee, and Sarah S. Richardson grapple with such implications, cautioning that many recent genetic studies have "revived the idea of racial categories as proxies for biological differences" (1). Similarly, in "Genetic Kinship," Nash charges that when geneticists merely declare that racial categories are not genetic but socially constructed, they all-too-conveniently absolve themselves of coming to grips with racist blowback and other consequences. The rhetoric of media texts that describe or utilize genetic ancestry are similarly implicated.

A fifth question explored in this book concerns how the economics, marketing, and cross-marketing of family history media and services forged by commercial and other enterprises and institutions inflect these issues and how they might represent a clear and present danger to privacy. Critical in this regard is the "Mormon" Church of Jesus Christ of Latter-day Saints (LDS), whose history includes structural racial discrimination (see Goodstein), as a perennial player in genealogy culture. The Mormons' genealogical preoccupation, which for decades has provided genealogical tools, texts, and services not otherwise readily available, derives from its doctrine that the identification and proxy baptism of deceased ancestors into the church facilitates the uniting or "sealing" of extended families in the afterlife (see Otterstrom). Conversely, Ancestry.com, while inspired by LDS genealogical interests, is the largest *commercial* entity related to genealogy. Media outlets and publishers producing genealogy-related texts and Internet-based genetic ancestry services also deserve scrutiny as integral players within the crossbred institutional cultures of genealogy, as do pertinent marketing discourses, blogs, and websites featuring tutorials, access to documents, information, promotions, user interaction, and/or the posting and sharing of family trees. Also significant are controversies related to the digital availability of genealogical and genetic ancestry information that could be data mined, ultimately violating the privacy of consumers in ways that could negatively affect their lives, including in racially manifested ways (see Cooke; Creet; Shanks).

The final question I explore here concerns the media landscape on which family history texts, practices, and institutions now function: What can we learn about convergent, digital, and social media and the social relations by which they operate by interrogating their function and role in this context? Calculating the critical potential of genealogy cultures mobilizes theory and research addressing today's new media environment. This is even more crucial since genealogy practitioners perceive a "chasm" between the newer world of digital, record-based genealogy and earlier interpersonal forms of genealogy in which information flows from living relatives whose experiences of identity come into play (see "Chasm"). Where the digital divide relates to race, then, "pre-chasm" genealogy might hold sway for disenfranchised groups if only out of necessity. How might one account for this divide in the context of "new" media theory?

Following sociologist Manuel Castells's argument in *The Internet Galaxy*, sociologist Barry Wellman contends that *networked individualism* alters notions of community, a phenomenon that predates the digital age but has subsequently accelerated. In his view, people are connected as individuals who "switch rapidly between their social networks to obtain information, collaboration, orders, support, sociability and a sense of belonging" (16). In contrast to technologically deterministic stances, Wellman adopts a social constructionist view of media technologies, arguing that social networks of various kinds have always existed. Accordingly, technologies are not, in and of themselves, responsible for social change but constitute "powerful environments that enable people to manage their identity performances and their relationships" according to "specific affordances that contribute to the construction of unique communication environments" (Comunello xiii).

In 2012, Lee Rainie of the Pew Research Center and Wellman published *Networked*, a volume that elucidates the impact of networked individualism on interpersonal relations, including family connections. The authors aver that no digital media "technologies are isolated—or isolating—systems," although the individual, rather than social groups (including the family) in which he/she might be subsumed, is the core of his/her "social network operating system" (locations 333–46). Citing Castells's four cultures of the Internet—*techno-elites, hackers, virtual communitarians,* and *entrepreneurs* (see *Internet*)—Rainie and Wellman relate virtual communitarians to networked individuals, contending that neither group is self-indulgent. Rather, the concepts embed organizing, collective activism, and meaning making. Providing additional fodder for applying such ideas to family history media and culture, Rainie and Wellman claim that "densely knit family" is not the factor it once was and that "far-flung, less tight, more diverse personal networks" are the mainstay (location 441).

While Rainie and Wellman entertain networked individualism's capacity for social change, including its dystopian possibilities, they mostly render the concept in ideologically neutral terms. They assume a world in which access to technology and the ability to use it are effectively unhampered by age, race, class, gender, and other factors. Just as I did in "'No Politics Here': Age and Gender in Soap Opera 'Cyberfandom,'" Asian studies scholar Lisa Nakamura points to the fallacious assumptions of a 1996 MCI ad touting the Internet as blind to differences of race, gender, age, and infirmity. Just because people are not necessarily visible when participating in social media does not mean that the marginal identities they inhabit are not rendered as hegemonically online as they are offline or that anonymity does not embolden bigoted users. Hence, to account for these differences, theories introduced in this and other chapters serve to "criticalize" networked individualism and adapt it to the study's goals.

Ultimately, the volume determines whether a critical genealogy around issues of race, ethnicity, and intersectional identities is imaginable given the media-infused tools, texts, practices, cultural contexts, and technologies currently mobilized. After all, Kramer concurs that genealogy aids identity formation and that genealogy "functions as a tool through which the ties of genetic kinship can be both acknowledged *and* disavowed" in the course of critically navigating relations of power ("Kinship" 393). The Latin origins of the word *radical* associate it with the planting of "roots"—in Italian, *radici*—information that helps to clarify the multiple meanings of this book's title.

OBJECTS OF ANALYSIS

Answering these six questions requires examining genealogical practices, participatory cultures, institutions, marketing, tools, documents, and other texts in a mediated, multicultural context. While I have not explored every book, video, website, blog, or social media reference to genealogy in racial or ethnic terms, I have focused on many of these sources that are most visible, indispensable, and/or pertinent to the study's issues. For instance, while "how to" books on genealogy abound, the study pinpoints Bryan Sykes's *The Seven Daughters of Eve* (2001), a key contribution to the field of genetic ancestry that helped popularize this science even before 2003, when the human genome was fully mapped and genetic ancestry testing services began to proliferate. The study builds on Catherine Nash's critical reading of *Seven Daughters* in "Genetic Kinship" and explores the book's reception in light of its relevance to identities of gender and race and the privileging of biological over cultural forms of relatedness. In similar terms, I explore a book turned documentary, Spencer Wells's *The Journey of Man: A Genetic Odyssey* (2002). Wells, a geneticist, now heads the Genographic Project, a scientifically oriented genetic ancestry testing service. Recipients of the testing often post online discourses in response to the information they receive, and there are now YouTube uploads that racialize selected populations using genetic ancestry science and those in which users discuss DNA results that suggest racial hybridity in their genetic ancestry. Such posts can generate controversy, as is evident in user responses, accounts in other texts and discourses, and emerging debates related to privacy and the data mining of genealogy and genetic ancestry information (see Creet).

Scrutiny of the LDS church and other genealogy-linked organizations is vital. In this regard, the study interrogates official websites, marketing, product output, and controversies involving privacy. I also examine the institutions and texts of television, particularly in light of twenty-first-century series exploring racial and ethnic identity in family history and responses to this programming.

The most noteworthy early example of family history television was ABC's dramatic 1977 miniseries *Roots*, adapted from Alex Haley's 1976 historical novel of the African American experience derived from his own genealogy. In the twenty-first century, this genre has expanded to include the BBC's *Who Do You Think You Are?*, which debuted in 2004, and numerous international versions. A partnership among actor Lisa Kudrow, Ancestry.com, and others produces the US adaptation (NBC, 2010–12; TLC 2013–). In addition, since 2006, PBS has broadcast four miniseries/series hosted by Harvard literature professor Henry Louis Gates Jr.—*African American Lives*, *African American Lives 2*, *Faces of America*, and *Finding Your Roots*. And in 2013, PBS began airing a version of an Irish series, *Genealogy Roadshow* (RTÉ), loosely based on *Antiques Roadshow* (BBC/PBS). Using various genealogists and interviewers, the PBS production travels to various cities and presents solutions to ancestry mysteries submitted by noncelebrity locals. Produced by Brigham Young University Television (BYUtv) under LDS auspices, *The Generations Project* (2010–12) profiled one noncelebrity guest per episode. *Family Tree*, a mockumentary sitcom series, aired on HBO in 2013. A young half-Irish Brit, Tom Chadwick (Chris O'Dowd), is motivated to research his genealogy when an elderly aunt passes away and leaves him a box of mementos. Two programs introduced in 2016, BYUtv's *Relative Race* and TLC's *Long Lost Family*, mimic popular forms of reality television and mobilize issues of racial and ethnic identity as they pertain to defining and legitimating kinship.

My genealogical journey has taken me not only into the world of genetic ancestry testing but also physically and/or virtually around the country and to my ancestral homeland. I have examined the racial/ethnic experiences of my forebears, positioning them within larger, cross-cultural contexts; visited family history sites; participated in family history tourism; attended family reunions; conversed with family members young and old, close and distant; and gathered and/or perused mediated documentation in engaging with genealogical institutions. As Timothy asserts, members of diasporic groups consider making pilgrimages to be part of their genealogical endeavors. Nakamura, however, counters that "travel and tourism, like networking technology, are commodities that define the privileged" (17). Where class intersects with race, then, both tourism and digital participation are affected. Nonetheless, institutional, procedural, interpersonal, and documentary experiences involving "roots tourism," in-person and technologically mediated encounters with family members and genealogy-related organizations, the everyday performance of family history, and involvement with genetic ancestry testing are instrumental in pursuing the inquiry's aims.

APPROACHES AND METHODS

This volume is primarily a work of critical media and cultural studies. However, it employs historical, textual, and particularly ethnographic methods while applying a compatible blend of critical theory and insights from disciplinary and interdisciplinary fields, including communication, digital media, film, television, American, memory, kinship, migration, and heritage studies as well as sociology, education, anthropology, history, genetics, and geography.[1] Hence, the word *media* in the volume's title signifies a many-featured landscape of cultural institutions, texts, practices, and communication channels.

Virtual ethnography of participation in genealogy cultures, including scrutiny of online responses to mediated and other genealogical texts and related services, proceeds from previous research. In *Serial Monogamy*, which explored cybercultural reception practices related to daytime television along with its texts and institutional structures and processes, I sought to refine protocols for *virtual* ethnographic audience analysis—in the broader sense, analysis of participatory media cultures on the Internet. Drawing on an early version of Thomas Lindlof and Bryan Taylor's *Qualitative Communication Research Methods* and Christine Hine's *Virtual Ethnography*, I carved out an approach using multisited virtual ethnography to assess online commentary. I selected discourses by prominence, via keyword searches based on relevant issues, and via an adapted method of *snowball sampling* in which the discourses of subjects on one site revealed the pertinence and significance of those on another. Virtual ethnography has more recently come to be known as *netnography*, a term coined by Robert V. Kozinets in his book by that title, in which he outlines an approach that incorporates techniques from his fields of marketing and public relations. In this volume, I expand my earlier approach by interspersing my autoethnographic experiences, findings, encounters, and insights. Otherwise, I am a nonparticipating critic in analyzing the digital cultures of family history.

My father and I both took one DNA test, and I took two others as part of the autoethnography and alongside the dissection of ethnic and racial identity in genetic ancestry as depicted in genealogy media and read by audience members. I compare and contrast providers in terms of their presentation of information and results and implications for identity, such as whether one recognizes race and kinship as biological or cultural, as well as in terms of racial hybridity.

I decode personal documents, images, and video related to my family history, in some cases using Kuhn's scheme for analyzing texts of memory derived from the work of cultural studies pioneer Raymond Williams on *structures of feeling*. Williams explains that a structure of feeling emerges from attempts to make sense out of "impulse, restraint, and tone; specifically affective elements of consciousness and relationships" and "their connections in a generation or period" (132–33). Kuhn's ruminations on the significance of personal memories and memory texts reference such structures and dovetail with her concept of *collective imagination*, which occurs when people resistively connect their personal memories to collective understandings (165–66). Accordingly, Kuhn suggests deconstructing memory texts such as photographs by gauging of shifts in focus between the individual and the historical collective and/or between historical and ongoing injustices (8).

For this and other autoethnographic facets of the inquiry, I adapt sociologist Leon Anderson's *analytic autoethnography* approach, which has certain critical features: (1) "member-researcher" status, which in this case means that I am thoroughly immersed in the various family history practices under scrutiny; (2) reflexivity in the analytic process, which in this case means that I take my subjectivities and competencies into account; (3) transparent visibility of the researcher in the investigational narrative, in that the reader of this work is advised of my participation; (4) interplay with other perspectives, in that I supplement my personal journey with perspectives drawn from netnographic data; and (5) substantial theoretical analysis (378). The study's application of this approach occupies a middle ground between those who want to limit the focus on personal transformation (e.g., Atkinson) and those who contend that too much "distanced theorizing" dilutes the intimacy of autoethnography (Ellis and Bochner 433). The volume peppers autoethnographic insights throughout, as modeled by Kuhn's invocation and assessment of personal experiences and mementos in *Family Secrets*. The autoethnographic component of the study reflects members of a generation who are seeking to take stock of their lives; coming to grips with inevitable mortality; dealing with the declining health of parents; reinvigorating interest in racial, ethnic, national, and other identities; and reconnecting with far-flung histories and family members via social networks and both old and new media. This component also unearths pivot points of thought and action in the performance and representation of family history that can be adapted by others and facilitated by digital media.

CHAPTER PREVIEW

Chapter 2 gauges hegemonic and/or resistive meanings, readings, or outcomes in or related to traditional and digital media institutions, tools, texts, practices, participatory cultures, and identities associated with taking up and/or performing genealogy. It scrutinizes issues of privacy, race, ethnicity, class, age, and intersected identities in such terms. The chapter highlights genealogical tourism and family reunions in light of the racial/ethnic dimensions of my autoethnographic sojourns. It also elaborates existing theory and research on social and digital media and situates these insights in terms of day-to-day practices of genealogy. Subsequent chapters address particular issues concerning digital and social media.

The third and fourth chapters interpret discourses of postidentity, race/ethnicity, and their intersections with gender and class in terms of salient issues and historical contexts such as slavery, Jim Crow, immigration, and similar circumstances represented in twenty-first-century family history TV and its reception, which is analyzed via ethnographic (including virtual ethnographic) investigation. The chapters incorporate autoethnographic experiences and insights with regard to the processes, tools, and outcomes of genealogical practices, considering their bearing on the investigation's critical trajectory, as well as the implications of racial, ethnic, and intersected modalities of identity as inferred from genealogical documents.

Chapters 5 and 6 assess genetic ancestry texts and practices. Chapter 5 considers television and other traditional media treatments of issues related to race/ethnicity and intersected identities, hybridity, and racism and racialization as well as the unique "brick walls" facing descendants of slaves in tracing their genealogy and the ways that genetic ancestry operates in these circumstances. Chapter 6 explores digital media's role in terms of these issues and others, such as the definition of kinship, addressing testing service providers, YouTube videos, the virtual interplay of participants, and my autoethnographic experiences with genetic ancestry.

The concluding chapter melds findings from throughout the study with overarching autoethnographic insights. Utilizing and supplementing Kuhn's scheme for analyzing texts of memory, I dissect and contextualize genealogical information and mementos such as family photographs and video in terms of the issues and theoretical framework of the study. I reflect on my attempts to envision and narrate a cultural moment in my grandmother's immigrant family and the lives and identity-intersected experiences of my four Italian great-grandmothers according to general and (to the extent possible) particular knowledge, pivoting between details known and un-known. I reflexively assess these efforts in terms of the seeming conflict between individual and collective perspectives. I present my conclusions concerning digital/social/convergent media and suggest amendments to existing theory, noting relatively unexplored issues that can nonetheless create missing, incomplete, and/or atypical branches on the family tree, such as LGBT identities and intersections, adoption and other forms of family building that might be racially transgressive, wrong turns, and unexpected or sensitive revelations. Such phenomena can both present obstacles and create critical opportunities. I also contemplate genealogy media and culture in international contexts and suggest avenues for future scholarship, recom-mending strategies for the recuperation of racial/ethnic and intersected identities that emerge through connecting the practice of family history to historical and contemporary social issues.

UNRAVELING
GENEALOGY CULTURE

THE ROOTS OF ROOTS

Anthony Ferguson and Warrick Chin note that the veneration of ancestors and early printing technologies combined to encourage the Chinese to record the pedigrees of royals and nobles dating back before the modern age. Genealogy developed in European societies as a means of establishing lines of succession and inheritance among the wealthy and noble (see Weil; Silberman and Purser). In both cases, such pedigrees, inheritances, and/or lines of succession tended to be patrilineal or otherwise preferential toward males. Somewhat later, other social classes were included, and in Asia, these practices extended into Korea, Vietnam, and other places where Chinese migrations and/or influence came to bear (see Ferguson and Chin). My sister-in-law recently visited her family's ancestral site in Vietnam, where genealogical artifacts dating back centuries were left untouched as a consequence of superstition despite the communists' ascendance. However, this is not always the case with such Asian artifacts.

François Weil focuses on the "transformation in America of a European conception of kin" after the seventeenth century (locations 85–88): "Some Americans saw in genealogy the means to preserve family unity and kin consciousness; others had religious reasons to explore their roots; still others hoped to reinforce their social pretentions with an illustrious family tree; many put genealogy at the service of their racial and exclusive purposes" (locations 91–93). However, Weil also chronicles a slow but steady shift that achieved momentum in the mid-twentieth century: "It took decades, the civil rights movement, and the new interest in ethnicity and heritage for American genealogical culture—popular, multicultural, and multiracial family history—to settle in" (locations 121–24).

Nancy Shute's 2002 article in the *Smithsonian* magazine credits the influence of the 1977 television miniseries *Roots* (ABC), based on Alex Haley's 1976 novel, in which the story is modeled on his family's "up from slavery" narrative. According to both Shute and Weil, *Roots* prompted African Americans to pursue family history and endeavor to scale the "brick walls" that the historical fact of slavery often presents. Haley's work, however, drew challenge.[1] Nevertheless, Shute and Weil tout Haley's role in building racial/ethnic awareness and pride that helped spur Americans' interest in genealogy and their own racial/ethnic backgrounds. In 2016, a remake of *Roots* aired on the History Channel.

In the isolated island country of Iceland, populated by just over three hundred thousand people descended from a small band of Vikings, early genealogies were recorded in the *Íslendingabók* (*Book of Icelanders*). A website emerged out of efforts begun in 1988 to digitize and update these genealogies, eventually resulting in a new *Íslendingabók* established in 1997 by deCODE Genetics in collaboration with the programmer who digitized the old one. Icelanders now have access to an app that enables them to bump cell phones to determine whether they are second cousins in order to avoid dating close family members (see Khazan). deCODE has generated important science about genetic mutations causing disease within this relatively homogeneous population by linking *Íslendingabók* information and citizens' medical records. Iceland's preeminence in these areas became a vehicle for recuperating national pride after the country's financial collapse in 2008 (see Creet). However, some Icelanders began protesting the use of their medical records without consent, and Iceland's Supreme Court agreed (see Creet; Shanks). Iceland is a nutshell case in which corporate entities' access to genealogical, genetic, and health-related personal information could lead down a slippery slope.

UNDERSTANDING THE INSTITUTIONAL MATRIX

Douglas Kellner, a political economist of media, recommends *multiperspectival* study looking at various facets of the communication process. In the case of genealogy culture, this approach also applies with respect to cultural practices in which media involvement has become more and more vital. When it comes to genealogy, political economic examination of key players in terms of their interrelationships, imperatives, and mediated cross-fertilization, whether commercial or otherwise, becomes crucial.

The doctrine of the Church of Jesus Christ of Latter-day Saints (LDS), which preaches that only baptized members can unite in the afterlife, has courted controversy, despite the church's insistence that departed souls will reject unwanted baptisms (see Stone; Levenson). Lists of the deceased awaiting baptism have previously included Holocaust victims, although in 1995, church officials met with Jewish leaders and agreed to discontinue baptizing such victims. However, disputes continue over the baptism of murdered journalist Daniel Pearl and others whose families find the practice to be a violation. For some, use of LDS genealogical materials and services in light of such practices may present serious ethical questions. For others, including me, an utter lack belief in the premises underlying and efficacy of these practices means that any moral qualms are outweighed by the value of using these materials to educate and illuminate.

Many local LDS churches have Family History Centers, which are free for public use and offer reference materials, computers, microfilm readers and scanners, and other items appropriate to the service population. Many provide free access to Ancestry.com, its affiliates, and other sites. The LDS church's open-access FamilySearch.org website links organically to Family History Centers and offers tutorials, family trees, and other information; for nominal shipping costs, patrons can have microfilm or other material from the main LDS Family History Library in Salt Lake City, Utah, delivered to local Family History Centers for onsite usage. Mostly between 1938 and 1963, the church dispatched its missionaries to microfilm vital records from around the world and has since been working to digitize those materials as well as to collect additional sources in more than forty countries (see Shute). Microfilm and other materials not kept at the main library are stored at the church's Granite Mountain Records Vault near Salt Lake City.

The LDS church and the affiliated Brigham Young University have produced or coproduced three genealogy-related television programs. Hosted by FamilySearch.org, the annual RootsTech convention is held each year in Salt Lake City. The church has also created GEDCOM (Genealogical Data Communication), a universal and completely transferable digital format for text-based genealogical data.

Although a private, commercial venture, Ancestry.com emerged in 1990 when two Brigham Young University graduates, Paul B. Allen and Dan Taggart, began dispensing CD-ROMs containing genealogy information that had been collected by the LDS church. Affiliates of Ancestry.com include RootsWeb.com, Genealogy.com, and MyFamily.com, among others, and documentary TV series related to family history often consult the site and count the company as a sponsor. The site allows free posting of family trees, which generate additional data that can attract subscribers. Monthly or yearly subscribers can also access documents from the site's archives. While Ancestry.com and LDS genealogical services are ostensibly independent of one another, Julia Creet's documentary, *Need to Know: Ancestry and the Business of Family*, features LDS representatives suggesting that Ancestry.com's continued success is in their interest.

The site's information, especially subscribers' family trees that incorporate personal photos and documents, presents a privacy concern. Users can prevent other patrons—but not the company or its affiliates—from accessing personal family tree information, and that access continues in perpetuity, even if patrons removes their trees from the site or restrict the viewing of information about living persons. This privacy issue extends to other genealogical sites and services—in particular, genetic ancestry testing services such as 23andMe that include health-related analysis, some of which can be linked to race or ethnicity (see Creet). Ancestry.com also operates AncestryDNA, a genetic-ancestry testing service that does not provide health-related analysis but is still implicated in related controversies over privacy and data mining.

Prior to 2015, Ancestry.com offered Family Tree Maker, proprietary and fully integrated family-tree-building software. However, the company discontinued the program and phased out associated services. This has the effect of prompting more family historians to house their trees on the site and thus provide Ancestry with access to additional subscribers and increase the company's control over genealogical sharing among family members (see Cooke). Ancestry.com subsequently entered into an agreement with the company distributing RootsMagic, another genealogy software program, designed to achieve transferability from and ultimately produce a new Family Tree Maker.

MyHeritage.com, which has had relationships with both Family Tree DNA and 23andMe genetic-ancestry testing services, is the primary alternative to Ancestry.com. Founded in 2003 by Gilad Japhet, MyHeritage.com is a private company headquartered in Israel. In 2016, it launched its own genetic genealogy service, MyHeritage DNA. Like Ancestry, it allows patrons to post family trees without charge but requires a paid subscription to access documents. MyHeritage.com has its own integrated, proprietary software, Family Tree Builder. Additional media producers and service providers, their commercial and other imperatives, their interrelationships with one another, and related issues and controversies are discussed later in the volume.

NAVIGATING THE WHO, WHEN, AND WHY

Few studies of genealogical practices investigate multiple demographic variables, particularly in terms of race, ethnicity, intersected identities, and/or motivations and uses of digital media. The most recent study cited by scholars was performed by Maritz Research in 2000 and found that 60 percent of Americans were interested in family history, an upsurge from 45 percent in 1995. The study also unearthed various impetuses for taking up the hobby, such as hearing family stories, talking to others involved in family history, and attending family reunions. Significant percentages of subjects had constructed a family tree or visited an ancestral locale, and a third had utilized the Internet in their research. Since the study was proprietary, other details, including demographic makeup (other than a roughly even split between men and women) and demographic variations in response, if studied at all, were not released.

When it comes to practices of genealogy, the *who* question is somewhat related to the *why*. Because I am the only one of my siblings who does not have children and because I do research for a living, solitary time and expertise have clearly been factors in my participation. Communication scholar Ronald Bishop's 2008 article, "In the Grand Scheme of Things," is based on a qualitative survey of family historians and turned up similar motivations. "I feel obligated," one subject answered, "because I have the desire, skills, and the time, to continue my family research, organize it, and share it" (397). However, for me, these are not the only inducements. The fact that I do not have children means that I am more likely to seek out other mechanisms for contributing to future generations of my family. Even aging parents share these motivations. Another of Bishop's subjects noted, "I am happy to pass on what I have learned to my children, knowing that my descendants will know a lot about their ancestors because of my efforts" (398). Scholar of social work S. Brady Umfleet found cause and effect reversed in this regard, concluding that when older adults engaged in family history over the long term, their sense of *generativity*, or concern for posterity and future generations (see Erikson), increased. In addition to feeling an obligation to chronicle family history for posterity, Bishop's respondents also felt pride in producing accurate family history narratives.

Although Bishop's survey was not concerned with demographics, age appeared to be a factor in taking up genealogical practice. One subject commented that genealogy was an activity that an older person can "easily," manage while another remarked that it made "mortality easy to take" and meant that his progeny might "keep [him] alive in their family histories" ("Grand Scheme" 398). Eric Wee touts the increasing interest in genealogy and the growing participation of aging baby boomers and contends that a "sense of mortality" plays a role in this surge (A1). Shute makes similar claims and refers to the 2000 Maritz survey.

After James Tanner made a live presentation at a genealogy conference, he reflected, "I looked out on an audience where the vast majority were well along in years.... So why is this the case? Where has the public relations for genealogy gone wrong? It should be noted that genealogy or doing research are not listed as 'Selected Leisure Activities' by the U.S. Census Bureau.... So, as a society we do not value the type of activities involved in doing family research, especially in our 'spare time.'" On another family history website, Thomas MacEntee observed that conferences attract "mostly women (70%) and mostly age 50 and above" ("Age Demographic") and suggested that although conferences that lack a social media angle may fail to attract young people, they may indeed conduct and/or confer about family history when social media are integral. He also observed that the first season of the US version of the genealogy TV series *Who Do You Think You Are?* (NBC, 2010) did not profile celebrities under age forty. Though he is correct on the latter point, it is not clear that more youthful faces on these series would stimulate interest among the young. In addition, most young adults (including celebrities) tend to be oriented more toward the future than the past, looking to build their careers and to create their own families. Celebrities are likely to receive more lucrative career-building offers than appearing on family history shows. Otherwise, the political economy of commercial television favors collecting a younger audience, and even PBS is concerned with expanding its adult audience in a more youthful direction (see Mook).

Cardell Jacobson, Phillip Kunz, and Melanie Conlin's 1989 sociological study found that among the young, women were better able than men to identify elders on both sides of their family trees. Ronald Lambert's 1996 study of temporal factors in genealogical practice also demonstrated that women had a higher level of interest in the role of family historian.

Table 2.1 shows the overall demographics of profiled celebrities on the US versions of various genealogy programs. The data show that *Who Do You Think You Are?* has included some younger guests since the first season, though older celebrities remain vastly in the majority. Most of the uptick occurred after 2013, when the series moved from NBC to the Learning Channel (TLC), a subsidiary of Discovery Communications, after failing to garner sufficient ratings, particularly among viewers aged between eighteen and

TABLE 2.1: DEMOGRAPHICS OF PROFILED CELEBRITIES ON US FAMILY HISTORY TELEVISION SERIES										
				Age*		Race/Ethnicity**				Gay/Bi***
Program	# Profiles	Men	Women	39 or Younger	Forty or Older	Black	Latina/o	Asian	Middle Eastern/ Native American	
Who Do You Think You Are? (NBC/ TLC, 2010–May 2017) 68	26	42	14	24	54	9	1	1	0	6
African American Lives (PBS, 2006)****	9	5	4	0	9	9	0	0	1	0
African American Lives 2 (PBS, 2008)****	12	6	6	0	12	12	0	0	0	0
Faces of America (PBS, 2010)	12	6	6	2	10	2	1	2	3	0
Finding Your Roots (PBS, 2012–May 2017)	80	45	35	10	70	27	8	7	4	5

Notes: * Based on the celebrity's age at the end of the year of initial US airing.
** Racial/ethnic identifications based on a celebrity's primary identification(s) outside and within the program, not revelations made during the program.
*** Gay or bisexual status counted if based on publicly available, reputable information and/or indicated within the program.
**** Includes profiles of host Henry Louis Gates Jr.

forty-nine. In 2008, officials at TLC concocted a "Life Surprises" programming and marketing theme that transformed the cable channel from emphasizing home improvement into a haven for sensationalized reality fare focusing on nonstandard families (see Silman). TLC programmers may have thought that a family history program would attract some of the same viewers who tuned in to see such controversial offerings as *Here Comes Honey Boo Boo* and *19 Kids and Counting*. As on these reality shows, as of May 2017 the TLC version of *Who Do You Think You Are?* has featured predominantly white faces, profiling only three African Americans, one Asian, and one Latina/o. The TLC profiles have, however, featured more women. A large majority of the celebrities profiled in the PBS series have also been older than forty. Mostly thanks to two miniseries devoted to African American family history, the PBS programs have proportionately represented blacks but have offered fewer profiles of members of other racial minorities (though more than on *Who Do You Think You Are?*).

Bishop's subjects "tended to downplay the importance of status and wealth to their family narratives" ("Grand Scheme" 402), a point echoed throughout the genealogical community. A quotation from American poet, actor, peace-activist, environmentalist, and genealogist Laurence Overmire frequently adorns genealogy websites and appears in Genealogy Word Art, a digital family history scrapbooking "kit" by LLL Creations: "History remembers only the celebrated. Genealogy remembers them all." However, as Mark Twain supposedly countered long ago, "Why waste your money looking up your family tree? Just go into politics, and your opponents will do it for you."

Genealogy can be an expensive hobby, depending on how and to what extent it is pursued. Both Lisa Nakamura and sociologist Kevin Meethan recognize a divide in which only advanced economies or the economically privileged attain sufficient access to digital technologies that can be used to collect data for genealogy purposes. This suggests that a swath of inhabitants in the Global South and elsewhere would likely not be in a position to engage in digital family history. Moreover, family history requires free time, which is also at a premium for the less affluent.

A report of attendance at the 2015 RootsTech conference and accompanying Innovator Summit reveals certain intriguing demographic data (see "RootsTech"). While RootsTech attracted 66 percent women and 34 percent men, these numbers were reversed at the more technologically oriented Innovator Summit, reproducing a stereotype and divide in which male-ness supposedly predicts comfort with digital technology (see Woods). At RootsTech, 57 percent of attendees were over age fifty-six, while the participants in the Innovator Summit were roughly evenly divided among the four age categories between eighteen and sixty-five; however, only 8 percent were older than sixty-five. The vast majority of RootsTech attendees counted themselves as "beginner" or "intermediate" practitioners, while the majority of Summit attendees identified as "intermediate" or "advanced, expert, or professional." Most RootsTech attendees described themselves as possessing "intermediate" technological know-how, while an even larger majority of Summit attendees belonged to the "advanced, expert, or developer" grouping. RootsTech attracted people from thirty-nine countries, while participants at the Innovator Summit came from eleven countries. No data were provided on race or economic class.

REENVISIONING THE HOW

The technological turn in genealogy involves more than digital divides related to age, class, and other aspects of identity. It is also associated with a divide referred to as "the chasm" by many committed genealogy practitioners (see "The Chasm"). Such practitioners assume a dichotomy between "post-chasm" genealogy (which transpires primarily via the use of digital databases) and "pre-chasm" genealogy (more interpersonal, intimate storytelling). The distinction between genealogy and family history may relate to this dichotomy, as the latter is more devoted to larger contexts that entail the weaving of narratives and hence the transmission of experiences that might relate to racial/ethnic identity. Meethan does not specifically refer to "chasm" discourses but nevertheless recognizes the split between oral and documentary memory in the writing of history (see Freeman): "the interplay between written and oral sources is complex and dynamic" and involves "balancing the archival traces of institutions with the personal narratives of self and other kin" (Meethan 103, 106). The dichotomous metaphor of the chasm, however, seems to mirror Rainie and Wellman's assertion that networked individualism deemphasizes "densely knit family" and foregrounds "far-flung, less tight, more diverse personal networks" (location 441). They also acknowledge networked individualism's capacity for collective activism and social change, two things for which digital/social media are today among the most powerful engines.

However, where genealogy is concerned, the chasm metaphor is overly simplistic. It is difficult to imagine a practitioner whose work does not begin with and remain aware of family narratives, whether or not it does so in whole or in part through digital/social media. However, while family narratives are invaluable, they are not immune to amendment based on documentation acquired through digital archives. Travel to brick-and-mortar archival sites occasioning interaction with librarians, genealogists, and others may also result in changes to family narratives.

My mother and her siblings understood from their elders that their paternal grandmother died in childbirth and passed this story on to their progeny. As a teenager, however, I asked my grandfather about his mother's death, and he abruptly put me off. I found his reaction odd, and when I began doing the family history and obtained my great-grandmother's death certificate, I discovered that she died of "carcinoma of uterus." There is no way to know whether he really believed that his mother died in childbirth or whether he simply gave that explanation to his children because gynecological matters were a taboo subject for an Italian American male born in 1896 (who, I later learned, arrived in the United States *in* his mother's uterus). The family history narrative now encompasses the prior understanding, the official cause of death, and these speculations. Moreover, such narratives are essential in unearthing issues related to marginal identities.

Genealogy thus does not seem to suffer from an unbridgeable chasm between traditional, interpersonal methods and the use of digital media; rather they are complementary, and I used all of these sources in compiling my family history narrative. An explanation for the persistence of chasm discourses might be that some practitioners, particularly older ones, have fallen behind on the digital end and lack the will and/or means to catch up. Moreover, the fact that digital archives simplify amateurs' access to information threatens the livelihood of longtime professionals. Even though one of Bishop's respondents opined that "computers need to work better for people without a lot of skills" and another remarked that entering data was a "boring occupation" ("Grand Scheme" 406), subjects seemed to use digital media as well as older means of record keeping, such as three-ring binders. In fact, a retired respondent of Meethan's credited newly acquired "free time" and digital/social media for stimulating enthusiasm for family history: "The computer really opened it up after I found out about 'mailing lists' & all the help and advice available from people on them" (107).

It is still important to evaluate the use of digital and social media around genealogical texts and practices. In particular, it is pivotal to interrogate the neutral terms in which Rainie and Wellman present *networked individualism* as well as the direction of activism and social change it fosters. Working from a feminist perspective, media scholar Amy Hasinoff warns that digital media research should "pay more attention to communication technologies' messy interconnections with people, context, social structures, and power" (272). Critics of networked individualism, in particular, observe Rainie and Wellman's ultimate failure to situate the concept in relation to prevailing hegemonic regimes. In the words of sociologist Jenny Davis, "I wanted the discussion of surveillance ... to engage with Foucault; I wanted discussions of the digital divide to be framed with theories of race, class, gender, and their intersections; I wanted discussions of self and identity." As journalist Andrea Miconi declares, "As long as we focus on networks, we can certainly gain an understanding of everyday practices, but . . . we should probably wait for more solid theories to be proposed that take power issues into due consideration. The shift toward network analysis can actually pose a very serious risk: that of forgetting the importance of the main social operating system of modern history—social class" (958). Leaving aside the question of whether social class is the one and only "main social operating system" that requires scrutiny, Rainie and Wellman's framework indeed must be infused with critical theory in studies of the sort contemplated here.

In keeping with Wellman's notion of the networked individual as one who "becomes the portal" (9), this volume focuses on the extent to which such individuals' engagements with genealogy texts and related cultural practices using digital/social media might resistively facilitate or mitigate collective and contemporarily relevant views of power, representation, and struggle. It does so by applying feminist, political economic, postcolonial, critical race, and other schools of critical theory in tandem with Rainie and Wellman's conceptualization.

BROADENING THE TERRAIN: FAMILY HISTORY TOURISM

What scholars and others refer to as "heritage," "roots," or "ancestry" tourism can aid in seeking critical context in family history practices (see Timothy 115). Wellman's premise that social networks are nothing new is critical here, as communication using both face-to-face and a variety of mediated channels is integral to such tourism and its associated information collection. Travel might be limited to visits to genealogical libraries or archives to obtain information needed to build a family tree but can be as extensive as domestic or international sojourns to visit locales, historic sites, cemeteries, or dwellings associated with persons or groups represented in one's tree, at times using specialized travel and tourism services identified via digital media. One might also connect or reconnect with distant or rarely seen family members or attend family reunions. The tourism arms of many national, regional, and local governments are visible online and have become specifically attentive to such travelers and/or the sites they frequent (see Timothy 126–38). Nationalities and ethnicities studied in this regard include Pakistani (Ali and Holden), Ghanaian (Asiedu), Scottish (Basu), Croatian (Carter), Greek Cypriot (Dikomitis), Indian (Hannam), Jamaican (Horst), Lithuanian (Kelly), Chinese (Lew and Wong), and Vietnamese (Nguyen and King). Diasporic identity and family history tourism go hand in hand (see Timothy; Asiedu; Basu; Carter; Dikomitis; Hannam; Nguyen and King). According to Timothy, family history practitioners who are the "more visible targets of racism and bigotry" can "come to terms with the past through the cathartic intensity of family history travel," a practice vital in the "mediation of diasporic identities"

(129). Such travel may but does not necessarily invigorate ethnocentrism. Catherine Nash found that diasporic tourists in Ireland ultimately confronted a complex, multifaceted, and eye-opening state of affairs: "There is nothing fixed or predictable about the relationship between genealogy, diaspora, and nationhood. Genealogy can serve to anchor and protect exclusive national cultures. It can be used to rework the nation as hybrid and heterogeneous. It can uncover prenational cultural relationships . . . as well as enact contemporary transnational collective identities" ("Genealogical Identities" 47).

One of the first journeys in my second-wave genealogical project occurred in 2010, when a trip to New York City to see a Broadway show occasioned a visit to the Ellis Island Immigration Museum (since renamed the Ellis Island National Museum of Immigration and expanded to include immigration before 1892 and after 1954—that is, beyond the years when the Ellis Island Immigration Inspection Station was operational). The museum and its website are supported by the Statue of Liberty–Ellis Island Foundation.

I had already performed a free search at the foundation's website and located the ship's manifest logging my paternal grandmother's arrival in 1912, when she was six. Even this task had been difficult. I vaguely remembered my grandmother, who went by *Genevieve* in the United States, advising me, in her Brooklynese accent, that her Italian first name was *Jovaneena* and that her school should have translated it as *Joanna*. When I learned a little more Italian, I realized that the correct spelling was *Giovannina*. I was struck by the fact that, on the manifest, the names of all those in her party, including her mother and three of her five siblings, had *X* marks next to them (see figure 2.1, lines 13–17). Her father, eldest sister and brother, brother-in-law, and nephew had previously made crossings, although we believed that the eldest sister had remained in Italy. When I visited the museum, an attendant at the Family History Center explained to my sister and me that the *X* marks indicate that the person was detained for some reason. Learning the meaning of the *X* marks made our later audio tour of the holding area within the facility a bit weightier, as I envisioned my grandmother as a six-year-old girl as part of a diverse "huddled mass" of immigrants figuratively if not all literally in the same boat.

While at the Family History Center, I tried again to locate the ship's manifest for the arrival of my grandmother's father, which I had not been able to find. The attendant suggested that I search for his eldest son, who most likely had accompanied him. Success! We realized that an error had occurred in the indexing for the father, and the attendant flagged the record for correction by volunteers.

Figure 2.1: Ship's manifest listing members of the Barone family. The X marks indicate people who were detained, a group that includes Giovannina (my grandmother, line 16); her mother, Maria Urrico (incorrect spelling of Orrico); Giovannina's sister, Carolina; and their brothers, Giovanni and Luigi. Source: Statue of Liberty–Ellis Island Foundation.

In 2010, my father, then the early stages of Alzheimer's, expressed the desire to visit his childhood haunts and reconnect with the cousin who had been his childhood role model. The logistics of an overnight trip to New York with an Alzheimer's sufferer concerned me, but I acquiesced. We met up with my paternal second cousin, whom I had first encountered via Ancestry .com, at the Brooklyn cemetery where the remains of my father's paternal grandparents and four other family members lay under a single marker (see

Figure 2.2: Scuteri grave marker, Holy Cross Cemetery, Brooklyn, New York, where
my paternal-line great-grandparents and four other family members are buried.

figure 2.2), and we later visited my grandparents' gravesite. Bishop notes that
one of his respondents had become interested in genealogy after visiting a
cemetery where family members were buried ("Grand Scheme" 399).

We located my great-grandfather's house in what is now a mostly Asian
enclave in Brooklyn. Both my grandfather and my father were born in the
house, and great-granddad met his end in front of the building when he was
pummeled by a motorized beast, something he could only have imagined as a
child. The formerly tiny, one-story, flattop bungalow had become an upscale,
multiple-story home that Dad did not recognize, though he did recall the
building across the street, which had been an orphanage. My cousin knocked
on the door of my father's childhood home, and the current owner, an apparently Italian American woman, answered. When she learned that the elderly
man with us had been born in her house, she stepped out to meet him, and
she told us that she had just renovated the home. We stayed the night at the

Long Island home of one of Dad's maternal cousins, Bob, who traded war stories with Dad and with whom I practiced speaking rudimentary Italian and later discussed Lady Gaga, of all things. Bob's wife provided family albums from which they invited me to borrow photos for purposes of digitization.

On my first dedicated journey to Italy in 2011, I met in Rome with my Italian family contacts—second cousins once removed. My mother and some of her relations had met these brothers years earlier. Their father had helped reconcile the Italian and American branches of the family, as my mother's aunt had desired. I made contact with the pair through Facebook, mentioning that my mother had given me a copy of the handwritten patrilineal tree going back to the 1730s that their father had compiled as well as some related documents, including a letter to my mother from her aunt's son, who had been collecting information on the American branch of the family, and who wrote that he was ill and hoped that someone in the next generation would take over the job. Atop one of the seven hills, gazing down on the Eternal City, I surprised my Italian cousins with a letter that their father (since deceased) had written to one of them. One of my American cousins apparently had translated it, but, the addressee had never received it. He was quite moved.

The cousins confirmed something I already suspected—the family lore about our descent from nobility was not mere hearsay. Birth and marriage documents for the mother of my mother's paternal-line grandfather addressed her as *gentildonna* (gentlewoman). Her maiden name, Aragona, is indeed the name of a noble family in southern Italy. However, the question of whether she was descended from the Spanish House of Aragon remained unresolved.

Among our materials was a court record for the grandfather of my mother's (disinherited) paternal-line grandfather. In the mid-1800s, the ruling Bourbons in the south had imprisoned this ancestor for siding with those, mostly northerners, who fought to expel the Bourbons and unify Italy under a single government. After discussion with the cousins, I conducted further research about the politics of unification, its race/class intersections, and their links to the diaspora that led predominantly *poor* southern Italians—my immigrant ancestors—to flee. After we finished talking, my cousin took me back to my hotel on the back of his Vespa, a hair-raising but unforgettable ride through the streets of Rome.

Next, I headed south to visit two mountain towns from which some of my poorer progenitors came. The LDS church had not microfilmed records from the town in Campania that was home to my mother's maternal ancestors. A winding bus ride took me from the nearby city up to the *municipio* (town hall), where I encountered the same proprietary attitude that probably explained why the LDS missionaries had been denied access to the records. Even now, the caretaker permitted me to acquire only a transcription of information from the original, handwritten record and only for one generation beyond my great-grandparents. The caretaker did inform me that people from Brazil had recently been asking about their ancestors and that we apparently shared a set great-great-grandparents.

The second town, in Calabria, was the birthplace of my paternal grandmother and near the town from which my mother's paternal lineage comes. After another bus ride up a mountain, I found these city hall employees a bit more enthusiastic about answering my queries and providing me with copies of key documents. In addition, they were entertained by my sketchy Italian. I already had my grandmother's birth record, which surprised the caretaker, who wanted to know how I had acquired it. I explained that *molti anni fa* (many years ago) people from a family history library had taken photos of the town's records. Additional documents obtained here helped me resolve a mystery concerning my grandmother's parents, who had married in the town but apparently had been born in a nearby village. Learning its name later enabled me to return to the LDS microfilm and trace these lineages further into the past. I considered walking to the address where my grandmother was born, about three kilometers from the office, but time constraints and precarious terrain prevented me from going. Overall, my 2011 visit to Italy raised as many issues as it resolved, particularly concerning the interrelationships among the politics and economics of unification, southern Italy, and the diaspora.

In the summer of 2014, my sister and I returned to that same town in Calabria where our paternal grandmother was born. After searching online, I had found a US-based tour service run by a woman of Calabrian heritage that catered to genealogy tourism in that region. Before we traveled, I had emailed the tour service documents that might help with my specific questions regarding denizens of the town. Among these matters was the birthplace of my great-grandfather's mother, who I could not find in the LDS's microfilmed birth or marriage records for the town documents. I thought her death certificate might clear up this matter, but microfilm from the town ends in 1910, and she likely passed away after that. According to our tour guide, a group of documents that might contain her death record had been lost or destroyed. I do know, however, that her maiden name seems to emanate from northeastern Italy.

Figure 2.3: Facebook post featuring the unoccupied structure in southern Italy where my grandmother was born.

I also wondered about my grandmother Genevieve's eldest sister, known by her middle name, Rosa, who we were told had died in the 1917–18 influenza pandemic. I had not been able to find a marriage record for her, and we had assumed by witnessing discussions of her death that she had remained with her husband in Italy. My father vaguely recalled that her daughter, Margherita, had visited when he was a child and was able to supply a surname that might belong to Rosa's husband. The tour guide found a marriage record showing that Rosa had married a man by that surname at the age of fifteen. Armed with these names, I later discovered that they had made the crossing to the United States a year before my grandmother. The guide escorted us to the home of a middle-aged couple who knew the cousin who had visited my father. According to the couple, although the cousin had lived for a time in Italy, she had been born in the United States, and her husband was kin to the current mayor. They knew the names of her children, who had settled in the United States, but nothing about her mother's death.

We then visited the unoccupied structure where my grandmother was born, although the addresses on the units had changed, making it difficult to determine exactly where this event took place. As we stood in the parking area of the building, my sister and I heard a worker on the site bellow

"Mannaggia!" (Damn!) and instantly knew we were in the right place. We had frequently heard this expletive, with exactly the same inflection, in my grandparents' house. We took photos of the building (see figure 2.3), had lunch at a local trattoria, and toured the provincial capital, Cosenza. When I remarked to our tour guide that everyone had been so friendly, he explained that tourists from the north seldom visited because "they think we're all Mafia." This observation figured into in my subsequent research concerning the history of the north/south divide, its racial and economic components, and its relationship to migration, whether to, from, or within Italy.

Figure 2.3 is typical of the photos that my sister and I took on this trip. Media researcher Larissa Hjorth argues that women's use of phone cameras to chronicle their travel experiences on social media has generational components. As middle-aged women, our reticence to include ourselves in the pictures was not surprising. Data collected by researchers at Selfiecity.net show that women under age forty take more selfies than men. Older women, however, appear to have so internalized cultural messages about their fading physical appeal that they do not want to "spoil" the beauty of the scenery with images of themselves.

The only other family history stop on our trip was unplanned. As we waited for our Italian cousin to show us some of the less touristy nooks and crannies of Rome, it began to rain. We ducked into a special exhibit on emigration from Italy inside the Victor Emmanuel II Monument complex. The exhibit helped us understand the scope of the diaspora that occurred in the late 1800s and early 1900s, highlighting major destinations elsewhere in Europe, in Latin America (Argentina, Uruguay, Brazil), and in Oceania (Australia) as well as the United States and Canada. As a consequence of the emigration to Latin America, individuals with ancestral heritages matching those of many Italian Americans fall within the Hispanic or Latino/a racialized minority group. An interactive installation allowed patrons to search for emigrants' names, and I conversed with the attendant who later emailed me a link to an Italian website where digitized embarkation records were available.

In 2015, as I arranged to attend the Mile High Big Italian Cousins Family Reunion near Denver, I decided to take a detour to Salt Lake City to visit the LDS Family History Library. Bishop describes a survey subject who "happened to stop in Salt Lake City" with his wife and popped into this library, took an orientation class, and just began searching ("Grand Scheme" 399). This experience prompted the couple to pursue family history research on their future trips. In my case, having LDS microfilm readily available and state-of-the-art equipment on which to view it was a luxury. Although

Figure 2.4: Faces on display outside the LDS Family History Library in Salt Lake City, Utah, including one Mexican, one Native American, and one black male.

Mexican, Native American, and black male faces were included in a display in front of the library inviting patrons and passersby to "Discover Your Heritage" (see figure 2.4), few of the faces inside appeared nonwhite. Most of the people posted at information desks were friendly volunteers, and although some of the volunteers who work at my local Family History Centers are non-Mormon, identification badges seemed to indicate that those here were indeed church members.

On the surface, the Family History Library appeared much like a public institution; however, at one point I overheard a volunteer tell a patron that the record she was perusing indicated that her ancestor was simultaneously married to multiple women. In addition, a couple of volunteers were disconcerted when I asked where I might find books and reference materials about *who* has engaged in genealogy and *why*. One volunteer wondered whether I was referring to "how to" materials and eventually remarked that my question was a first. For volunteers, at least, the answers to those questions are contained in the church doctrine itself. Indeed, the library does not hold a copy of François Weil's *Family Trees*, the most recent book that addresses such issues from a historical perspective. In contrast, Weil's book is generally available at the genealogy arms of public institutions such as the Seattle Public Library, the Newberry Library in Chicago, and the New York City Public Library.

This chapter's brief history of the development of genealogy in various parts of the world and examination of the demographics, motives, and extramural activities of practitioners provide a foundation for unraveling the intricacies of genealogical texts and practices. With this background understanding of the issues involving media and information technology that affect genealogy as well as commercial imperatives, controversies, and interconnections, I now turn to my family history journey and an analysis of media texts of family history and genetic ancestry, audience/participant responses, and related practices.

3

TUBULAR GENEALOGY I

Race, Ethnicity, and Intersectional Identities in Family History
Television and Related Practices

SURVEYING GENEALOGY TV

Investigating racial/ethnic identity, hybridity, intersectionality, and postidentity discourses in family history television series airing in the United States since 2000, their reception, and related tools, texts, and practices entails examining representations of relevant historical events, regimes, controversies, and roadblocks in genealogical practice. Although genealogy has been seen as a solitary, self-involved, and often elitist pursuit carrying at best the potential to make associations between the personal and history, television texts could theoretically not only link individuals to history but also discover associations and/or disassociations between histories as well as between historical and ongoing relations of power.

Alex Haley's *Roots* has been considered a major influence on genealogy culture. Argues Nancy Shute, "The impact of *Roots* on genealogy and popular understanding of African-American history" remains undeniable (78). As both François Weil and Shute chronicle, *Roots* spurred an interest in genealogy not only among African Americans but also among other Americans eager to establish their identities within a multicultural context.

This multicultural dimension creates an *opening* for considering genealogy-related texts and practices as something more than straightforward reaffirmations of gender, race, and class hierarchies. In most European traditions, establishing patrilineal inheritance and ethnic/class purity were for centuries the chief impetuses for keeping records and fashioning family trees (see Silberman and Purser).

In any case, the surge of multicultural interest in family history sparked by *Roots* preceded and set the stage for the digital genealogy boom and the array of family history TV programs airing in the United States today. The descendants of African slaves often refer to their progenitors as "Kunta Kinte ancestors," after the analogous Haley forebear in *Roots*. That term is used in the genealogy miniseries/series hosted on PBS by Henry Louis Gates Jr. Twenty years after the premiere of *Roots*, PBS and Brigham Young University coproduced *Ancestors* (1997), a documentary series focusing on records available to amateur genealogists.

Who Do You Think You Are? was the first twenty-first-century genealogical series to make a splash, airing in the United Kingdom starting in 2004 on BBC2 and subsequently migrating to BBC1. Along the way, it has inspired international adaptations from Israel to Portugal to Russia to South Africa and more. The US version, produced by *Friends* costar Lisa Kudrow along with Ancestry.com and other partners, ran for three seasons (2010–12) on NBC before moving to TLC (2013–).

"Mediatizing Memory," Anne-Marie Kramer's study of the UK version of the show, grapples with, among other things, the criticisms put forth by the British press, which "focused on whether the programme, and genealogy in general, offered an opportunity to engage more fully with history" or "simply represented a "self-indulgent 'navel-gazing' identity project" (442). Kudrow has been frank about the program's goal to "personalize history," as she stated on a 2 September 2013 episode of the syndicated daytime talk show *Live with Kelly and Michael*. Kudrow's words echo Kramer's pronouncement that genealogy's role is to "personalise the past" (qtd. in Amot), but fails to express, as Annette Kuhn explicitly does, that such memory work has potential to reach "far beyond the personal" (5).

Episodes of *Who Do You Think You Are?* typically open with a male narrator's voice-over bio of the celebrity subject of the profile, who then details his/her motivations for engaging in family history and contacts relatives for documents, photos, and/or other data by which to supposedly "establish" one or two previously vetted lineages to study. The celebrity then follows the trail(s) backward, chronicling his/her progress to the camera at critical junctures, traveling to key sites, and meeting with local genealogists who have set the stage for further "revelations." Voice-overs by the narrator fill in historical context as documentary images (writings, drawings, paintings, photos) flood the screen, and most episodes end with the celebrity summing up his/her genealogical journey to family members. In the United States, Ancestry.com is also a major sponsor, and the series explicitly uses

Ancestry's digital services. It also features genetic testing by AncestryDNA in a few episodes highlighting African American celebrities.

In the various PBS family history miniseries/series hosted by Henry Louis Gates Jr.—*African American Lives* (2006), *African American Lives 2* (2008), *Faces of America* (2010), and *Finding Your Roots* (2012–)—Gates presents the guest with a "Book of Life" that the show has compiled and then leads the guest through its contents with the instruction, "Please turn the page." The role of this book becomes more explicit in the latter two programs. In the majority of instances, only Gates and/or local informants appear in remote locations uncovering material for this book. Gates provides bios of guests as their profiles commence and narrates historical context throughout. All of the series use Ancestry.com, while a couple of episodes feature the LDS Family History Library in Utah, with Gates explaining its raison d'être in *Finding Your Roots*. When they aired as well as on DVD, episodes of the Gates-hosted shows are bookended by family-history-themed corporate sponsorship ads from such entities as Ancestry.com and AncestryDNA as well by family-themed ads from otherwise unrelated consumer products such as Coca-Cola and McDonalds. The PBS series reflect more racial and ethnic diversity than the other genealogy programs, but all of these shows are deficient in terms of profiling celebrities under the age of forty (see chapter 2).

African American Lives and *African American Lives 2* each depict seven or eight African American notables in addition to Gates, while *African American Lives 2* also features an "average person." The family histories of these subjects are presented across four episodes that move backward in time. The first episode highlights the twentieth century, including Jim Crow and the Great Migration from the rural South to northern cities; the second addresses emancipation and Reconstruction; the third covers the period of slavery; and the fourth explores the Middle Passage and attempts to establish deeper roots through genetic ancestry. DNA testing also occurs in *Faces of America* and *Finding Your Roots*, which profile celebrated persons of diverse backgrounds. The four episodes of *Faces of America* feature profiles of twelve Americans representing various racial, ethnic, and/or immigrant groups, with each person appearing in between one and three episodes. *Finding Your Roots* aired in alternate, even-numbered years until the 2017 season, with each season including ten installments and more than twenty profiles, mostly of American notables. However, the 2012 season also featured a noncelebrity friend of Gates. Each episode focuses on two or three particular guests, usually connected by a common thread.

BYUtv's *The Generations Project* debuted in 2010 and ended its run after three seasons; this examination focuses on the final season. This series is distinct from most other genealogy profile programs in that it features "average" people, thereby mitigating the class bias in genealogy generally (because the wealthy leave longer paper trails) and in genealogy series specifically (because celebrity profiles seem automatically to reproduce myths of reliably upward mobility and to undermine efforts to foreground genealogy's associations with the everyday). However, the show does not necessarily exploit this distinction in a manner that contests hegemonic orientations of ethnicity, race, or their intersectional affinities.

The Generations Project features Ancestry.com, the LDS Family History Library in Utah, local Family History Centers, and occasionally genetic ancestry. Each episode is titled by the guest's first name and begins with that person outlining a personal concern that he/she believes will be assuaged by calling on the fortitude of ancestors, in line with BYUtv's slogan that it "helps you see the good in the world." Given its low budget, *The Generations Project* seldom features exotic locations or ventures back more than a few generations. Subjects travel and, with the help of relatives and local genealogists, narrate their own stories before returning home. A separate interviewer/narrator appeared in earlier seasons. Despite the apparent LDS background of some of its subjects, the series avoids highlighting the baptism of the dead as a motivation for genealogical inquiry. Moreover, the family trees that are displayed do not reflect the polygamy practiced by LDS males during the mid- to late nineteenth and early twentieth centuries.

The PBS adaptation (2013–) of the 2011 Irish miniseries *Genealogy Roadshow* also features noncelebrities. Its format, in which the production travels from US city to US city to answer the previously solicited family history questions of relatively diverse individuals, often tends to explore whether a familial relationship exists between the profiled party and a notable person or a connection exists between a notable historical event and a family member. However, the series also explores idiosyncratic family mysteries, and genetic ancestry is occasionally used. The show's tendency to focus on biological connections to big names diminishes the potential offered by the focus on noncelebrity guests in that programs profiling well-known individuals automatically validate post-orientations. Narration, much of which relates to local or regional histories, fills in context for many queries.

In addition to a voice-over narrator, featured genealogists recite history as they interact with the profiled guests. These genealogists include Kenyatta

Berry, the African American president of the Association of Professional Genealogists; D. Joshua Taylor, president of the Federation of Genealogical Societies; and, beginning in the second season (2015), Mary Tedesco, a specialist in Italian genealogy. The hosts share their discoveries while seated with the guest at a desk or small table holding a tablet or computer. In season 1, the guest's family and interested onlookers encircle the small table, and an interviewer follows up with a short debriefing in which the guest relates her/his experience. In the second season, the genealogist and client meet either inside or outside a public building, amid the hustle and bustle of many patrons apparently also seeking information about their roots.

When questions involving remote locations and histories arise on the program, no depictions of travel outside the immediate production zone occur during the first season, although a few such instances involving only a host occur in the second season. There is an assumption that the show's experts may have supplemented information directly gathered via digital media by contacting colleagues in other localities. These elements can create a claustrophobic aura around practices of genealogy that may discourage mind- and place-expanding firsthand engagements. On one hand, this situation reflects the networked individualism that Barry Wellman posits in "Little Boxes" by visually depicting the genealogist as the center point, networking outward to resolve various issues. On the other hand, this approach contests the aspect of networked individualism in which nonmediated interactions that may require travel and other kinds of mediated interactions are part of the same network arrangement. The show undoubtedly had only a shoestring budget for the four episodes of the first season but seemed better funded as the second season took shape.

HBO's *Family Tree*, a mockumentary sitcom, began airing its eight episodes in 2013 and was not renewed for a second season. It was created by British actor/producer Jim Piddock and dual American/British citizen Christopher Guest, well known for writing, directing, and acting in film mockumentaries such as *This Is Spinal Tap* (1984) and *Best in Show* (2000). In it, a thirty-year-old Brit of half-Irish heritage, Tom Chadwick (Chris O'Dowd) begins tracing his genealogy using clues found in items inherited from an aunt and at points begins to suspect that he possesses racial/ethnic hybridity. The show focuses less on visiting libraries, archives, and websites than on physically encountering contacts in the United Kingdom, Ireland, and the United States who have some connection to or knowledge of his forebears.

Wendy Davis writes, "As its name suggests, the mockumentary is constructed using the documentary style, and it mocks both the characters and

scenarios it presents, as well as documentary's traditional, social, realist functions" (1). Other examples of mockumentary sitcoms include the UK and US
versions of *The Office* and the US series *Modern Family.* The mockumentary
sitcom eschews both the live and canned laughter traditionally associated
with the sitcom genre and incorporates conventions of cinema verité and/or
other documentary styles, such as having the characters speak to the camera
in interview mode. *Family Tree* also contains improvised dialogue. The series
appears to mostly satirize *Who Do You Think You Are?*, in that acquiring
photos and other artifacts from family members sets off the genealogical
journeys in both programs.

The 2016 genealogy series draw from conventions of existing reality TV
fare, perhaps to connect with younger demographics comfortable with these
conventions. Based on the ITV British series of the same title, each episode
of TLC's *Long Lost Family*, cosponsored by Ancestry.com, unites or reunites
two relatively diverse noncelebrity guests with one or more biologically
related family members such as birth parents, birth siblings, or a family
member given up for adoption. Shepherded by Chris Jacobs and Lisa Joyner,
two white hosts who have unraveled their own adoption mysteries, genetic
testing via AncestryDNA and/or conventional research using Ancestry.com
facilitate the quest.

BYUtv loosely models *Relative Race* on a CBS reality show, *The Amazing
Race* (2001–). Four married couples compete for twenty-five thousand dollars
in prize money by taking a cross-country drive—in the first season, from San
Francisco to New York—using paper maps and burner phones but with no
GPS or Internet connectivity. Between the two urban centers, rural locations
in the Southwest, Mountain West, and South predominate in the first season
(three of the couples visited Utah). In each episode, the couples advance to
a new location and meet a challenge to receive specific directions to the
home of a previously unknown relation linked through genetic testing by
AncestryDNA and/or conventional means using Ancestry.com. Host Dan J.
Debenham, a former ESPN anchor, dishes out a strike in each episode to the
couple who most exceeds their allotted time in locating the family member.
Earning three strikes results in expulsion from the race.

The first season features contestants appearing to range in age from their
early twenties to early fifties. As might be expected from the LDS-affiliated
BYUtv, all couples are heterosexual. Seven out of eight contestants are white;
one white woman is married to an African American man. All surnames
are Anglo-Saxon. In the second season, the prize doubles, and a somewhat
younger and a bit more diverse set of contestants travels between Miami

and Boston. The "married" requirement automatically excludes blood/adoption-related family members from competing as a team and typically means that only four contestants make a genetic connection in each episode. The program displays a nativist bent in that the number of generations that a contestant's lineages have been in the United States can determine his/her degree of participation, at least in the family connection aspect of the race. Certain family lineages might receive short shrift because of a dearth of unknown, geographically dispersed, yet US-based relations. In the first season, two contestants do not make a genetic connection until the competition meets or crosses the Mississippi. One becomes so frustrated that she considers quitting, since her main purpose for competing is to collect remote family members to make up for her emotionally remote immediate family. The final episode in New York City does not involve meeting relatives; rather, contestants encounter the homes, grave sites, food, clothing, language, and other touchstones of long-ago ancestors. The couple that includes the African American contestant dons Bavarian costumes. Another finds a connection between an ancestor and John F. Kennedy. Austrian, German, and Irish are the featured backgrounds, and all of the ancestors arrived in the United States by the mid-nineteenth century. New York City, boundlessly diverse and a perpetual repository of youth and innovation, is relegated to history for this relatively homogeneous group of contestants, most of whose more recent ancestors presumably vacated it for places the program seems to frame as the "real" America. *Long Lost Family* and *Relative Race* largely implicate issues regarding the definition of family and the importance of *genetic* connection regardless of race.

WHOSE LINE IS IT ANYWAY?

When I began digging into my genealogy, all I had to go on was interpersonal knowledge and the Italian family tree of my mother's father. The branches of this tree included not only a doctor and notary but sundry landowners and businessmen and a political prisoner who aided the cause of Italian unification. The medical degree of my 2X great-grandfather and the court record of his father were attached to the handwritten tree. The couple's first born, my great-grandfather Francesco, who had studied to become a lawyer or a priest, depending on who tells it, was disinherited after his noble mother's death for marrying "beneath his station." Deprived of the class status that might have mitigated against racial animus on the part of their northern

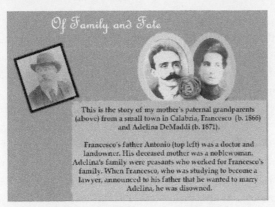

Figure 3.1: Portion of scrapbook page featuring my mother's paternal grand-parents and great-grandfather.

compatriots, Francesco and my great-grandmother, Adelina, emigrated to the United States in 1895 while she was pregnant with their third child, who would go on to become my grandfather (see figure 3.1). While their entry was legal, today my grandfather might be maligned as an "anchor baby," as would the woman he married, who also arrived in the United States from Italy in utero. Ten years later, after giving birth to my grandfather and three additional children, Adelina died at the age of thirty-four. In 1925, her widower petitioned to become a citizen, listing all of his children on his application. Searches using Francesco's name could not retrieve a final citizenship decree for Francesco or his Italian-born children, but his naturalization is indicated in the 1930 census.

Francesco lost all connections to his homeland, never remarried or learned a substantial amount of English, and spent time in a sanitarium before dying thirty years after his wife. Two of these great-grandparents' many descendants, and a descendant in utero, were among those killed in the attacks on the World Trade Center on 11 September 2001.

Despite the fact that my father's mother, Genevieve, was born in Italy, unlike my other grandparents, only through my mother's paternal grandfather could I apply for Italian citizenship under the principle of jus sanguinis (right of blood). My father's paternal grandfather was naturalized before 1912, and according to Italian law, birthright citizenship must come directly through an Italian citizen parent or an Italian citizen grandfather or great-grandfather along a parent's direct paternal line who did not alter his citizenship until after the birth of the next generation ancestor. However, because of another sexist quirk in the law, women (but not men) born prior to 1948, such as my mother or my father's younger sister, would be ineligible to apply for Italian citizenship through an Italian citizen *mother* or *maternal* grandfather. Yet on a 2016 episode of *Genealogy Roadshow*, a woman receives a document needed to achieve such citizenship from an Italian American genealogist who had acquired her own Italian passport through a similar process.

The saga of my mother's paternal grandparents is the earliest detailed family story I can tell accurately. My other immediate lineages (all southern Italian) contain the poor and dispossessed—peasant farmers (*contadini*), bricklayers, soil tillers, cowboys, spinners—meaning that it is extremely unlikely that there are any traces of them prior to the early nineteenth century, when pre-unification Italy began to keep civil records. Indeed, even after the advent of such recordkeeping, these people left relatively scant paper trails, and I must trace their collective plight only through broad historical inquiry and speculate about details of their personal stories.

A user discussing *African American Lives* on the forums of the Television without Pity website (now defunct) similarly and counterhegemonically acknowledged paper trail biases related to region and class, observing, "I know so much about my mother's side of the family . . . but on my father's side, nearly nothing. I also think that has to do with family circumstances—my mother's side are Northerners who were well-educated and were able to keep records and visit each other and my father's family were subsistence farmers who had to eke out a living in Mississippi."

Patrilineal naming and record keeping also make tracing *maternal* lines more challenging. In the nineteenth and early twentieth centuries, for instance, officials in Italian jurisdictions recorded the father's appearance at the town hall, to which he "delivered" the newborn to be legitimated by the male town official. The father is named at the top of the page, while the mother's name is buried much further down. The handwritten birth record for my father's maternal grandmother names her grandfathers but not her grandmothers. Moreover, these handwritten documents are often barely legible. (Since 1975, however, women in Italy retain their maiden names for legal and most other purposes.)

In the United States, census records, naturalization documents, and many other materials now available from online databases pertaining to married women rarely include their maiden names, complicating or even completely blocking genealogists' efforts to track maternal lineages. But such impediments pale compared to those in other areas: noted one poster on Television without Pity, "At least Americans have SOMETHING to work with. Try having a West Indian background where your parents start reminiscing about their grandparents sister 'Auntie Princess,' 'Auntie Baby' or 'Tanta' but have no knowledge of birth name." I overheard similar issues when a volunteer at the local Family History Center was attempting to help a patron of Jamaican heritage. These instances underscore the importance of area specialization among genealogists and volunteers operating in a multicultural context.

The intersected identity biases apparent through genealogical practice translate to family history TV. During much of European history, keeping records to document patrilineal inheritance for the wealthy and noble automatically connected race and class with gender. Not surprisingly, then, family history TV features copiously documented lineages leading to notable males. Revelation of this "ultimate ancestor" often signals a profile's closure.

Another respondent on Television without Pity criticized the premise behind *Who Do You Think You Are?* (2010, NBC): "Ugh, this is so stupid. Somebody who reproduced 200 years ago could have hundreds to thousands of descendants alive today, yet the descendant who becomes a celebrity has a special claim on the historical person's significance. Hey celebrities, if you want to discover how vapid and solipsistic you are just take a fucking poll." The same discussion thread featured a post complaining about actor Sarah Jessica Parker's "over-emoting in the first episode. She can't believe that one of her ancestors died of an illness in the CA gold rush! Or that another ancestor was accused of witchcraft in Salem! Well, sister, you have 1024 8th great-grandparents. One of them was bound to have had an interesting life." These reactions are resistive or counterhegemonic in that they bemoan the biases associated with the profiling of celebrities and/or emphasis on notable ancestors in family history television but are also hegemonic in their inherent assumptions regarding the significance of "celebrity" forebears over those who were ordinary people. Another participant in this conversation seemed to instinctively understand one mechanism behind Kuhn's counterhegemonic conceptualization of collective imagination: "It's difficult to connect to family members from the past when you know nothing about them other than they were anonymous farmers.... When you find out they lived during events mentioned in history books, you can get a better feel for what their lives were all about. That to me is exciting and I felt the same way when I found out about my own family history." Whether that excitement leads to an exploration of these historical contexts or to efforts to connect them to contemporary circumstances is, however, another matter.

On *Who Do You Think You Are?* (NBC, 2010), the profile of actor Brooke Shields based on her paternal pedigree leads through a pope's banker and concludes with an announcement of her ultimate ancestor, Henry IV of

France, and a sidebar pertaining to his grandson, Louis XIV. These connections seem to perplex Shields, as if she is wondering what this has to do with her life today. On *Finding Your Roots* (2012), actor Maggie Gyllenhaal's tree ends with Henry I of England through Swedish nobility on her father's side and revelation that she is genetically connected to four US presidents. The ultimate male ancestors of actors Ashley Judd (*Who Do You Think You Are?*, NBC, 2011) and Sally Field (*Finding Your Roots*, 2014) arrived on the *Mayflower*. The maternal lineage of African American poet Elizabeth Alexander (*Faces of America*) leads to England's John I and Charlemagne. On *Who Do You Think You Are?* (TLC, 2013), supermodel Cindy Crawford's genealogy is traced through nobles and kings of Italy, including Pippin and ultimately his father, Charlemagne. In fact, a generally accepted mathematical formula suggests that everyone with European heritage descends from Charlemagne (see Zimmer), a proposition not acknowledged on these programs (although they do use documentary evidence rather than math to establish the lineage). Commenting on Crawford's profile on Television without Pity, one user resistively mocked the elitism of the genealogist who identified the Charlemagne branch of Crawford's family tree: "Regional Genealogist: 'At first I was downhearted, because I knew you were coming all this way and [I] was going to have to tell you [that] you hit every branch on the bo-ring tree . . . and then I found old Ebenezer here, and suddenly you had yourself one high falutin' fancy pants tree!'"

A game of "Six Degrees of Kevin Bacon" transpires on an episode of *Finding Your Roots* (2012) featuring married actors Bacon and Kyra Sedgwick. Her profile includes her maternal Eastern European Jewish lineages but emphasizes the aristocratic Sedgwicks of Massachusetts, culminating with a signer of the Declaration of Independence. Bacon, who is descended from Edward I of England, is a cousin of Barack Obama, Brad Pitt, and . . . Kyra Sedgwick (though there is more than six degrees of separation).

Asians, too, can often locate pedigrees going back centuries and terminating with notable patriarchs. On *Finding Your Roots* (2012), the ultimate ancestor of half-Korean Rabbi Buchdahl founded the Chosun dynasty and existing pedigrees going back centuries and leading to male dynastic figures are also revealed to Korean American comedian Margaret Cho and CNN medical correspondent Sanjay Gupta, an Indian American. Chinese American cellist Yo-Yo Ma is also presented with just such a pedigree on *Faces of America*, while another going back ninety generations is delivered to Chef Ming Tsai on *Finding Your Roots* (2014). On *Finding Your Roots* (2012), Gates specifically identifies the genealogical paper trail bias as class-based without noting its relationship to gender or race.

On PBS's *Genealogy Roadshow*, the tendency for the noncelebrity guests to pose questions of relationship to a notable person suits the program's format. For example, on the Detroit episode in the first season, a Latina forgoes learning about indigenous and other, perhaps less prestigious forebears in favor of determining whether she is descended from Juan Ponce de León, the Spanish conquistador. (She is!) In the Nashville installment, two guests wonder whether they are descended from legendary frontiersman Davy Crockett, and another receives confirmation of her biological connection to a US president. In the Austin episode, a young Chicana eager to qualify as a Daughter of the Republic of Texas establishes descent from a forebear who fought for Texas against Mexico. In some instances, the resident genealogists are strikingly apologetic toward those whose suspicions of exalted lineage cannot be confirmed. A discussant on Television without Pity counterhegemonically concurs that this aspect of the series is not compelling: "The kind of quick shot—just tell me that I'm related to someone famous—is the part of genealogy shows that I find boring, and that was most of what this was."

Predictably, Tom Chadwick's journey on HBO's *Family Tree* follows the male ancestors in the Chadwick line. One of only two detours to explore female relations occurs when he investigates the life of his aunt, Victoria, who bequeathed to him the box of mementos. Much is made of the fact that Aunt Victoria was childless and apparently a lesbian; her failure to procreate unmistakably nudges Tom back to the "straight" and narrow patrilineal trail. Later, Tom discovers that his 2X great-grandfather, Civil War veteran Charles Chadwick, reversed what is typical (for Americans) and emigrated from the United States to England. Tom manages a trip to California to meet with distant cousins, only to discover that Charles moved because his family could not accept his relationship with Tom's 2X great-grandmother, Rebecca, who appears in a photograph to be Native American and thus inspires Tom's contact with the local Mojave tribe. His inclination to travel further along a maternal passage seemingly ends when he discovers that Rebecca was not Native American but rather Jewish.

RACE, HYBRIDITY, INFERENTIAL RACISM, AND POSTIDENTITY

Genealogy TV implicitly acknowledges intersections between race/ethnicity and class while striking a postidentity pose and finding intersections between race and gender impenetrable. The PBS celebrity profile shows are most intriguing in this regard, offering incisive narration of historical junctures pertinent to race and ethnicity. However, they profile successful people (even the "average person" in *African American Lives 2* is a college administrator), implying ease of upward mobility in a largely postfeminist, postclass, postracial society.

HBO's mockumentary sitcom *Family Tree* satirizes multicultural curiosity of the kind spurred by *Roots* in the genealogical profiles of guests—in particular, white guests—in family history television. After a photo fools Tom Chadwick into thinking that his patrilineal great-grandfather was a highly placed general, he finds that this ancestor was merely the photographer who took the picture. An actual photo of his great-grandfather then surfaces, but his appearance and garb suggest that he is Chinese. Tom's father, Keith (Michael McKean), is quite certain that his father and grandfather were not Chinese, remarking that blue eyes but not "Chinesity" can skip a generation. Conversely, the proprietor of the antique store, Mr. Pfister (Jim Piddock), antiessentially contends that family characteristics are as much cultural as biological and not always passed on: "My great-grandfather was German, but you don't see me annexing countries."

Tom soon discovers that his forebear was a small-time actor and that the photo was taken while he was in costume as Nanki-Poo, the male romantic lead in the "Japanese" cast of characters from Gilbert and Sullivan's satirical operetta *The Mikado*. As a child, I was similarly confused when tagging along to my mother's rehearsals for local theater performances of *The Mikado* and other Gilbert and Sullivan comic operas. Only somewhat later did I realize that *The Mikado*'s blatantly evocative character names (at various times, my mother played both Yum-Yum, the female lead, and her sidekick, Pitti-Sing) and some of its costumes were distinctly closer to Chinese than to Japanese. And I was older still when I understood that Gilbert's narrative was meant as a critique of his own culture and times and that the orientalist tinge of the piece is disturbing.

According to N. Kathy Lin, "'The Mikado' is a biting satire lampooning British government and society. We know from the outset that the Japan presented is too much of a caricature for the play to be truly about Japan. . . .

At a recent protest at Occidental College in California, students complained of distortions that are impossible to separate from the imperialist and racist attitudes of the time." Elaborating on Edward Said's *Orientalism* thesis, Lin declares that the Orient "has historically existed in the European (and Western) mind mainly in the form of an oppositional otherness," thereby justifying Western colonialism. Said himself wrote that the Orient was "almost a European invention, and had been since antiquity a place of romance, exotic beings ... remarkable experiences" (1). In her book about *The Mikado*'s cultural meanings, Josephine Lee concurs that the choice of Japan as the satirical setting du jour stemmed from England's late-nineteenth-century fixation on all things Japanese—and its hegemonic, colonial mind-set.

Family Tree offers a satirical take on the fascination surrounding the prospects of multicultural heritage—for instance, the reaction of Tom's family and friends to the potential for "Chinesity" in the family and the attendant conflation of Asian ethnicities and cultures. The show observes that when whites encounter multicultural ancestry on genealogy television (or in their own family history practices), they can cross the fine lines between complexity and caricature, esteem and fetishization, especially when appropriate context is absent. The ancestor in question may never be historically and culturally situated but rather can operate as a token or team mascot signifying American/Western exceptionalism and/or the profiled person's self-congratulatory open-mindedness.

Tom's short-lived burst of multicultural interest is revisited when he later comes to believe that his 2X great-grandmother was a member of the Mojave tribe. He visits the tribe to learn about its culture, only to discover that she was differently multicultural—that is, Jewish. We are also reminded of Britain's new multiculturalism by Keith Chadwick's ritual viewing of British television series DVDs, one of which is a family sitcom set in an Indian British household. Viewers seem to pick up on the fetishizing aspect of the series' multicultural content without necessarily countering it. For example, a commentator on Television without Pity said, "I think the thing I enjoy the most is how whenever Tom finds out something about his family, he jumps to assume the identity. Like how he said he could 'feel vibrations' when he thought he was Native American. (And then also admitted it could be due to his proximity to the London Underground)." Even if in a satirical vein, this British/American production whose action takes place on both sides of the pond appears to assume significance in terms of racial/ethnic hybridity and the increasing role of multicultural ancestry in stoking attention to genealogical practice.

Many narratives of genealogy television refer to movements, historical eras, and/or events in which race was pivotal. *Faces of America*'s profile of Olympic gold-medal-winning figure skater Kristi Yamaguchi chronicles the US internment of the Japanese-born and their families during World War II. Gates narrates and accompanies her to the camp where her father's family was held. The show discusses how Asians were prohibited from owning or leasing land and how the internees lost all of their possessions. Yamaguchi suggests that her race may have negatively impacted the endorsement deals she received. However, she won her medal in 1992, eighteen years before *Faces of America*, and the allusion to endorsement deals and her continuing visibility as a celebrity signal transcendence in postracial and postfeminist consumerist terms. On *The Generations Project* (2012), another Olympian, snowboarder Graham Watanabe, explores his paternal Japanese ancestry. However, the narrative skirts over internment and other histories of discrimination and exclusion.

Also on *The Generations Project*, Roi is an African American in his mid-thirties who admits to anger after seeing a white Hurricane Katrina refugee wearing a Confederate emblem. He is dubious when his mother wonders whether their forebears experienced "rejection" rather than bigotry. Another relative claims that "agency" was necessary for the family to endure under Jim Crow. Roi ultimately volunteers at a Baptist church in Joplin, Missouri, after the May 2011 tornadoes there. After helping to repair a white family's damaged home, Roi confesses that he "sweat out the anger."

Similarly, *The Generations Project* profiles white, middle-aged David, whose ambition and workaholism worry his family. As part of this mind-set, he fixates on a suspicion that ancestors left a dark-skinned child in Jamaica because they were "so determined to create a new life in Canada that they hid the fact that . . . they were black." A Canadian historian confirms the racist governmental policies that existed at the time. Visiting Jamaica, however, David realizes that his forbears did not abandon a child and cries with relief as the black genealogist assisting him reveals that she is his distant cousin. He returns home fetishistically sporting faux dreadlocks, relaxed and sated by knowing that his family cannot be personally implicated in racism. The segments on Roi and David postracially depict lingering doubts or resentments related to race as baseless, and peace and justice again emerge not from collective action or remedial policies but from private virtue, charitable acts, and/or personality adjustments.

A counterperspective is present but not affirmed in another *Generations Project* episode in which Eli Paintedcrow, an Iraq War veteran with posttraumatic stress disorder (PTSD), has reclaimed her indigenous heritage after realizing that she had become "the invader." "My history was taken from me," she attests, and she pursues it, in part, by seeking out her tribe in Mexico. However, there is no context offered for Paintedcrow's experiences or political viewpoints, rendering her inclusion on the show a relatively hollow exercise in diversity of the kind satirized by *Family Tree*. The episode fails to acknowledge that true diversity exists not simply from representing different bodies but rather from welcoming the diversity of perspectives that often accompanies that difference. The views Paintedcrow expresses on the program can easily be interpreted as one of several adverse symptoms of PTSD, as she is indelicately shown undergoing a PTSD episode halfway through the profile.

The fact that *The Generations Project* guests are mostly unknowns and that the 2012 season appears to more racially diverse than *Who Do You Think You Are?* may be strategic. While supporting Republican presidential candidate Mitt Romney, a member and former bishop in the LDS church, church leaders launched a public relations campaign featuring Mormons of various races. At the end of one key ad, each member of the diverse array voices the tagline, "And I'm a Mormon." Historically, however, the church had for many years overtly discriminated against blacks, banning them from the priesthood until 1978. As Laurie Goodstein outlined in the *New York Times*, the campaign emerged after participants in focus groups described Mormons with negative adjectives. The postracial subtext of some of the *Generations Project* profiles—"Leave resentment behind and follow us"—appears to correlate with this effort.

In other genealogy TV narratives, whites confront their ancestors' lives prior to and/or during the Civil War. On *Family Tree*, Tom ascertains that his 2X great-grandfather, Charles Chadwick, migrated from America to Britain after having fought in the US Civil War. Tom has a photo showing Charles in a Union uniform. However, when Tom contacts his American cousins by traditional media and journeys to see them in California, he discovers another picture in which Charles is wearing Confederate garb, and Tom's box holds buttons from both uniforms. He eventually determines from a letter that Charles may have impersonated a Rebel soldier to visit his sweetheart in Virginia.

One of Tom's American contacts invites him to join in a Civil War reenactment. Tom's career as a Union soldier is short-lived, however, as he is "killed" in the first minutes of the battle. His discomfort at the possibility that his ancestor may have fought for both sides—information he wants to "keep to himself"—persists in response to the earnestness, rigorous authenticity, and moral equivalency that govern cultural practices of Civil War reenactment in this text. After the event, he asks the man playing the losing Confederate general, "Is it hard to keep doing the same battles when you know you are on the wrong side?" The reenactor remains in character and rebukes Tom for his impertinence. More important, the contact who invited Tom to participate is playing the opposing Union general and is similarly not amused.

On *Finding Your Roots* (2012), New Orleans jazzman, crooner, and actor Harry Connick Jr., having learned his musical craft as a child from the family of his pal, African American jazz saxophonist Branford Marsalis, confesses that he "wanted to be black." He is happy to discover that his Irish immigrant forebears were not slave owners, but is dismayed to learn that one ancestor fought for the Confederacy. As a historian explains that many immigrants did so to avoid destitution, the camera lingers on the miniature Confederate battle flag propped alongside a similar US flag on the office floor (see figure 3.2), subtly signaling a connecting but otherwise unacknowledged thread between then and now. Connick is somewhat mollified, although he confesses that he had never wanted to know about his ancestors during the Civil War because such information was often unavailable to African Americans. Still, he quips that his next album will be "Negro spirituals." In response to Connick's profile, an Irish American commentator on the Television without Pity forums who had persistently contended that her immigrant group was more disadvantaged than many others, wrote,

> All my ancestors came from Ireland. Two were Confederates; one was Union. I don't feel the slightest drop of discomfort with the confederates in my family attic. They were beyond dirt-poor . . . and if they didn't die of some horrible disease right away, they often signed up with the Confederacy for the promise of money, food, clothing, etc. They also liked fighting a big bad superpower who was going to tell them what to do—in a sense, the U.S. Gov't became a substitute for the British.

This poster ignores the obvious "divide and conquer" strategies and inculcation of white privilege that contributed to Irish immigrant protests against the Civil War draft and demonstrates that knowledge of one's family history can fester in a hegemonic loading zone despite the interventions of genealogy TV. However, another Irish American poster responded: "In the interests of fairness and historical accuracy, people in power back in the 1850's and 1860's

Figure 3.2: In this screen shot from *Finding Your Roots* (PBS, airdate 25 March 2012), a Confederate battle flag is displayed alongside the US flag as a southern historian discusses the Confederate ancestor of Harry Connick Jr. Source: Kunhardt McGee Productions, Inkwell Films, and WNET, *Finding Your Roots* (PBS, 2012), DVD.

were happy to convert the Irish ignorance about slavery into a case of class warfare against slaves. . . . African-Americans and women and many immigrants were the tools of those in power in the 18th and 19th centuries. I am waiting for a show that highlights how the powerful retained their power." Family history television also ignores the race/class intersection involved in the Confederate Congress's 1862 Twenty Slave Law, which exempted owners who possessed twenty or more slaves (eventually changed to fifteen) from the draft. Highlighting this policy breaks down a residual belief that upholding slavery was somehow in the interest of poor whites.

On *Who Do You Think You Are?* (NBC, 2012), when country music artist Reba McEntire examines records showing that her 4X great-grandfather bought and sold slaves, including children, she wonders, "Why would you sell a child?" A southern white historian counsels her that whites cannot hide from the reality of slavery, proclaiming, "It's right in our pasts." Later, she makes a parallel to her 6X great-grandfather, who came to the United States as an indentured servant. She is quick to point out, however, that for him there was "a light at the end of the tunnel."

Also on *Who Do You Think You Are?*, southern chef Paula Deen confronts evidence of a slave-owning ancestor and exclaims, "Somebody took a bucket of cold water and threw it in my face!" She *personally* sympathizes with him, however, because he lost a son in the war and committed suicide after his plantation fell to ruin after emancipation. On 20 July 2013, Comedy Central's

The Daily Show referenced Deen's genealogical discovery after transcripts of a lawsuit surfaced containing allegations that she had once expressed a desire to throw a "plantation wedding" and an admission by Deen that she had used the "N word." Presumably as a consequence of these revelations, she lost her contract with the Food Network. Filtering the meaning of Deen's *Who Do You Think You Are?* episode through the prism of these more recent disclosures may intensify uneasiness with Deen's compassion for her slave-owning progenitor. However, at the time this episode aired, a Television without Pity poster freed Deen of any obligation to feel guilty about her ancestor's feet of clay:

> As a citizen, I think we all can feel the collective shame of slavery.... But to feel personally responsible for it because your ancestor took part in it is bull shit because that makes it about how YOU feel.... If I found out an ancestor owned slaves, what does that have to do with me personally? ... People are like that, having their own free will and stuff. Go figure. Paula would go back and tell him not to own slaves and that would make it all better? Please.

This response leans in a resistive direction in its repudiation of symbolic gestures but is hegemonic in ignoring the other side of the same coin. Deen appears personally to empathize with her forebear, a feeling that is analogous to experiencing guilt or shame on behalf of an ancestor despite the fact that one bears no responsibility for the ancestor's actions. Deen feels sorry for the fact that her ancestor lost his plantation and his son. However, the plantation was among the riches obtained on the backs of enslaved human beings, for whom the poster expects no sympathy from their owners' descendants.

On *Finding Your Roots* (2012), conservative Christian pastor Rick Warren makes a similar discovery. When Gates remarks that Scripture was often used to justify slavery, Warren responds defiantly that the Bible contains no such justification and admits that Scripture can be contorted to conform to one's personal views. The obvious, connection-making follow-up—to suggest that such contortions also occur in relation to the civil rights of others such as immigrants and LGBT persons—does not materialize.

A 2015 email authored by Gates and subsequently released by Wikileaks revealed that actor Ben Affleck was so mortified to discover a slave-owning ancestor that he asked to have that information omitted from his 2014 *Finding Your Roots* profile, and producers acquiesced (Alexander). During the Bacon/Sedgwick profile on *Finding Your Roots*, both are dismayed to realize that a northerner in their pedigree owned slaves. Gates visits a New England school and comments that northerners and some free blacks owned slaves, even though PBS genealogy program profiles suggest that free blacks did so in order to rescue family members from slavery to whites. Nonetheless, a black student reasons, "I might have owned slaves at the time." Bacon and Sedgwick are relieved to learn that their ancestors later repudiated slave ownership, and their reactions and those of other profiled persons in family history TV can be considered examples of Kramer's suggestion that genealogy often "functions as a tool through which the ties of genetic kinship can be both acknowledged *and* disavowed" ("Kinship" 303). In particular, on *Finding Your Roots* (2014), documentarian Ken Burns comments that a slave-owning progenitor who was beaten to death by one of his slaves certainly deserved what he got. Burns also disavows a forebear who was loyal to Britain during the American Revolution.

The Sedgwick profile also contains what Stuart Hall labels *inferential racism*, "those apparently naturalized representations of events and situations relating to race ... which have racist premis[es] and propositions inscribed in them as a set of *unquestioned assumptions*" ("Whites of Their Eyes" 83). One scene is reminiscent of the *white savior* or *antiracist white hero* trope (see Dantò; Cole; Madison), a manifestation of inferential racism in which the media "resituate whiteness as progressive and heroic" (Ono 228). In the scene, a Sedgwick family patriarch proudly tells Gates the story of Elizabeth "Mumbet" Freeman, a freed slave woman who worked long ago in the family home, where her portrait still hangs, and who is buried on its grounds.

The celebrity profiles on PBS's genealogy series also suggest that some white men maintained committed relationships with freed female slaves and that Native Americans also owned or returned slaves. This propensity to reassure viewers that white folks are not all bad and that blacks and Native Americans are not all blameless dovetails with broader issues. In a 2010 *New York Times* column, Gates urged President Barack Obama to shape the debate over reparations for slavery in that "African elites" as well as whites played a role in the slave trade (A27), just as Gates averred in *African American Lives 2*: "Africans sold other Africans." One of many rejoinders to Gates came from African American law professor Lolita Bucker Inniss, who forcefully asserted that whites created and perpetuated the slave market, regardless of who did the capturing (see Lisa Miller).

Postracism and the white savior trope are palpable in the 2012 *The Generations Project* episode titled "Amber," in which a white mother guides her mixed-race daughter in a quest to find her African American roots ostensibly without the assistance of the girl's absent "deadbeat" father and his closest kin, who refuse to help. The PBS celebrity profile shows dispel stereotypes by profiling successful people of color in a broad range of professions rather than just in the sports and entertainment fields. Indeed, Gates admitted in a 1 February 2006 NPR interview that he scrupulously worked against such stereotypes by selecting scientists, entrepreneurs, political and religious leaders, and authors for *African American Lives*. An ad for Ancestry.com in which a black man finds that his ancestor "was born a slave, but died a businessman" also avoids such stereotypes. However, such efforts can also be postracial fodder. Thus, noting more recent obstacles faced by nonwhite guests or their families might foreground race/class intersectionality and mitigate the otherwise postracial demeanor created by featuring luminaries.

Gates's activities drew challenge from another African American legal scholar after he defended rappers 2 Live Crew when they were charged with obscenity in 1990 . Kimberlé Crenshaw noted that Gates's defense of the rappers on the basis of African American culture failed to consider the blending of gender with race in terms of the group's contentious lyrics. Crenshaw was a key developer of feminist theories of intersectionality, and intersectionality is the basis of another critique of content related to African Americans in the PBS celebrity profile series.

Some of Gates's most uneasy moments in *African American Lives* and *African American Lives 2* involve the history and experiences of black women. On *African American Lives*, talk-show host/media mogul Oprah Winfrey discusses being raped at the age of nine and later molested by a cousin's boyfriend, abuse she allowed to continue to prevent him from battering the cousin. In response to this coercion, rape, and domestic violence, Gates can only say, "I'm sorry." The profile provides no intersectional context based in race and gender or race, gender, and class. In *African American Lives 2*, both Gates and actor Don Cheadle resist identifying with Cheadle's slave ancestor who bore a child by a white man while she had a slave mate. Gates expresses empathy, but not for the woman: "You could say you were married, but anyone could violate your wife." So if a gender/race intersection is at work in this incident, the gender in question is male. The programs also raise the issue of whether such unions could ever be consensual. On Television without Pity, a poster counterhegemonically maintained, "Relationships between slaves and slave owners can never really be consensual, IMHO. There may not be physical rape involved in all cases, but when the man holds all power over the woman (including selling her, her family, and her children away from each other) how can she be said to be making a free choice?" On

African American Lives 2, only actor/comedian Chris Rock, who appears in a subsequent episode, is definitive about consent being precluded by slavery: "If your kidnappers are lovely people, you've still been kidnapped." These texts exhibit a dearth of intersectional context for the perspectives and experiences of black women.

While the PBS celebrity profile series do a better job than *Who Do You Think You Are?*, *The Generations Project*, or *Genealogy Roadshow* in explaining the historical contexts and impacts of race-related events, policies, or periods in US history, most of these series purvey or allow postidentity orientations, reverence for genetic relatedness, inferential racism in the form of the white savior complex, inattention to race/gender intersectionality, and fetishization of hybridity.

INSTITUTIONAL FACTORS, AUDIENCES, AND SOCIAL MEDIA

Although many social media participants are only viewers of family history television series and not necessarily amateur genealogists, respondents on Television without Pity and various genealogy blogs make both hegemonic and counterhegemonic contributions via their interpretations of and/or reactions to the programs. However, even the counterhegemonic remarks reflecting Kuhn's collective imagination in terms of identifying with histories beyond one's own stop short of making recognizable connections to today's exigencies.

One reason for the apparent constraint is the corporate ownership of the discussion forums and social networking sites that have supplanted many of those instituted by fans and other noncorporate entities. For example, Bravo TV acquired Television without Pity in 2007. Despite the motto that appeared on the website's masthead—"Spare the snark, spoil the networks"—Television without Pity had instituted a controversial moderation system that included rules that inhibited controversy and maintained a certain level of comfort with the goal of keeping a wide swath of people content and coming back for more (see Hicks). I noticed the stifling effects of such moderation while collecting data. On one occasion, a moderator prevented participants from discussing whether a sexual encounter between the two main characters on the popular ABC series *Scandal* qualified as a rape, warning that this issue could only be discussed if the show itself explicitly labeled the incident as such. Many moderators were devotees of the shows being discussed and tended to employ their power as moderators to privilege their own textual interpretations and preferences. Mark Andrejevic concluded that Television without Pity had profited greatly from its users' participation, providing a platform for producers to exploit fan interactions for market research.

During a deliberation of the history of slavery inspired by the Gates-hosted family history series on PBS, a moderator posted, "Guys, the last time I checked, this thread was about a TV show. It's not a thread to discuss slavery in general, America in general, or the like. Discuss the show." Such reproaches undercut resistive trajectories or associations.

In early April 2014, Television without Pity closed up shop. Substantive social media discussions of TV thus have moved to other forums, all of which have their own limitations. On Twitter, for example, opinions were dispensed in 140 (later 280) characters or less, while official media pages on Facebook retain control over posts and topics for discussion.

It is difficult to draw conclusions concerning the larger digital/social media issues addressed in this volume, such as the implications of networked individualism for genealogical motivations and practices, based on social media participation pertaining to family history television alone. *Genealogy Roadshow*, with its claustrophobic focus on one city in each episode and adherence to a particular venue at this location, creates an aura of insularity around the social/digital media activities of the host genealogists. The celebrities profiled on family history documentary series have vetted genealogical profiles handed to them in a "Book of Life" or go through the motions of consulting Ancestry.com and/or a dusty document or two to "discover" the next clue to follow, although an assisting genealogist or librarian has clearly already done this. When average people are profiled on *The Generations Project*, their social media interactions are mostly of the face-to-face, interpersonal sort, as each thirty-minute episode spends little time on digital research.

The extent to which the members of the online audiences/users responding to family history television are at the center of a complex of digital media and/or other associations as Wellman's theorization of networked individualism might anticipate is difficult to determine in terms of genealogy, genealogy TV, TV generally, and/or an array of other identifications. However, the following chapter's consideration of race, ethnicity, and migration narratives as mobilized in/by family history television and other media, as well as additional autoethnographic insights based on social media responses, helps provide some missing pieces of the puzzle.

4

TUBULAR GENEALOGY II

Race, Ethnicity, and Intersectional Identities in Genealogy
Television Migration Narratives and Related Texts and Practices

THE "WRETCHED REFUSE"

For countless Americans, immigration is a potential site of discovery. Many
can document that one or more ancestors arrived between 1820 and 1924—
the so-called "Century of Immigration." The 1882 Chinese Exclusion Act
continued to bar immigration or naturalization by this group; otherwise,
regulation during this period occurred mostly at the state level. However,
escalating nativism led Congress to pass the 1917 Immigration Act, which
denied entry to adults who could not pass a literacy test in their own language, and ultimately the 1924 Johnson-Reed Act, which drastically restricted
entry by Southern and Eastern Europeans and prohibited Asian and African
immigration altogether.

    According to the ships' manifests available at the Ellis Island website and
Ancestry.com, my mother's paternal grandfather, Francesco, had seen America before he arrived in 1895 with his family to settle. Like many Italian men
contemplating migration, and like my other three great-grandfathers (in one
case, numerous times), he had checked things out in advance. A good many
other Italian men came and got work, sent money back to their families,
and then elected to return to their homeland permanently (see Mangione
and Morreale). Francesco's wife, Adelina, had a brother and sister who traveled to the United States in 1893, and he accompanied them. Their ship, the
Karamania, like most vessels carrying Italian immigrants to the New World,
set sail from Naples, which experienced an outbreak of cholera that resulted
in a protracted quarantine of the passengers before they were permitted to
disembark and pass through the recently opened Ellis Island facility. Even

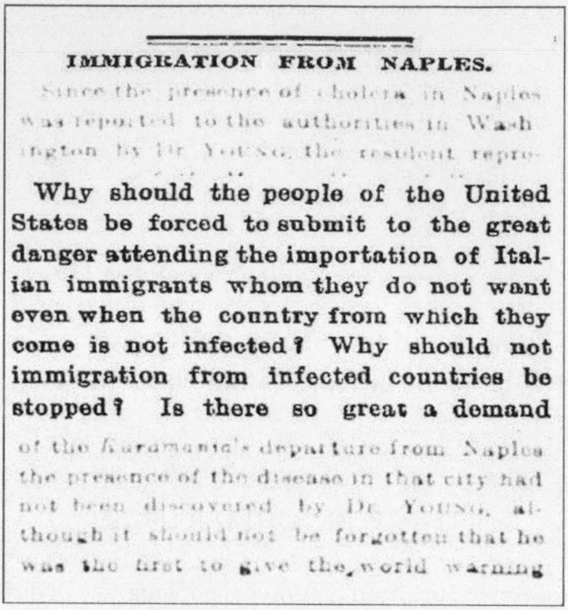

IMMIGRATION FROM NAPLES.

Since the presence of cholera in Naples
was reported to the authorities in Washington by Dr Youso, the resident repre-

Why should the people of the United
States be forced to submit to the great
danger attending the importation of Italian immigrants whom they do not want
even when the country from which they
come is not infected? Why should not
immigration from infected countries be
stopped? Is there so great a demand

of the Karamania's departure from Naples
the presence of the disease in that city had
not been discovered by Dr. Youso, although it should not be forgotten that he
was the first to give the world warning

Figure 4.1: *New York Times* editorial, 5 August 1893, reflecting nativist sentiment in response to the arrival of the *Karamania* from Naples, where a cholera outbreak had occurred. My great-grandfather was a passenger on this voyage.

though no cases of cholera developed onboard, the incident stoked nativist sentiment in the United States and provoked a 5 August 1893 *New York Times* editorial headlined "Immigration from Naples" (see figure 4.1). The editors asked, "Why should the people of the United States be forced to submit to the great danger attending the importation of immigrants whom they do not want even when the country from which they come is not infected?" (4). My great-grandfather, who unlike most Italian newcomers was educated and literate, although he never became fluent in English, might thus have learned for the first time that his well-heeled upbringing would not entirely shield him from ethnic prejudice.

In Henry Louis Gates Jr.'s prologue to the *Faces of America* episode featuring the "Century of Immigration," the 1924 cutoff point for the US immigration boom is not explained in terms of legislation limiting migration by certain groups, and the exclusion policies leveled against Asians and Africans are not spelled out. While a *Finding Your Roots* (2014) episode featuring singer/songwriter Carole King, playwright/screenwriter Tony Kushner, and attorney Alan Dershowitz notes restrictions limiting or turning away Jewish refugees fleeing the anti-Semitic Nazi regime in Germany in the 1930s, such information appears rarely, if at all, in the analyzed television texts. Despite the aura of romanticization surrounding the idea of the Century of Immigration, immigration stories might lead one to identify injustices that resulted in diasporas from many lands, injustices that immigrants found once they arrived, and injustices that newcomers still face. But are the immigration stories on family history TV likely to have this effect?

Echoing Nado Aveling's definition of *me-too-ism* (43), Christine Sleeter cautions that whites can be "uncritically ... ethnic in response to the identity work of people of color" (115)—for example, in failing to grasp that all experiences of racial or ethnic prejudice are not equal. Sleeter then goes on to show how she critically positioned herself to trace her own genealogy. While waiting for our local Family History Center in South Florida to open, another amateur genealogist and I got to talking about our discoveries regarding our ancestors after they came to the United States: she was amazed at how much discrimination her Irish ancestors had faced. She remarked on the inaccuracy of the popular image that immigrants saw the Statue of Liberty and suddenly everything was fine. Had we not been of the same (privileged) race, this could have been a *me-too-ism* moment. However, I made an association with my immigrant forebears from Italy and opined that newcomers "get a raw deal even now." Grimacing, she shot back with an exclusionary statement alleging that such discrimination no longer occurred. I cannot be sure that she was thinking primarily of immigrants of non-European origin, but since current controversies mostly reference groups of color (in South Florida, particularly Latin Americans and Haitians), it is a logical assumption. Therefore, she was engaging not in *me-too-ism* but even more problematically in *me-and-not-them-ism*. She was also coming from a postracial orientation.

Assimilation theories accounting for the acculturation of Century of Immigration newcomers are now largely rejected as ethnocentric and inadequate for today's multiracial circumstances (see Spickard). George Sanchez argues that in contrast to the earlier era, today's "racialized nativism" sets not only whites against nonwhites but nonwhites against each other (1009–10). Richard Alba and Victor Nee reorient assimilation to entail cultural change forged by immigrant groups and disagree that life was radically simpler for "European immigrants by their racial identification," since this claim imposes "contemporary racial perceptions on the past" (845). While circumstances are certainly different today, recognition of the ebb and flow of racializing discourses is pivotal, illuminating the constructedness of racial categories and highlighting the potential for development of new racial classifications that might give rise to newly defined racist policies. Such recognition also could provide openings to make illuminating, resistive comparisons and contrasts between personal and collective histories and between history and today's immigration politics.

Theorization regarding *racialization* is crucial to critiquing family history television's immigration narratives as well as discourses related to genetic ancestry. Michael Omi and Howard Winant describe *racial formation* as "the sociohistorical process by which racial categories are created, inhabited, transformed, and destroyed," noting that "race is a matter of both social structure and cultural representation" (55–56). Following Omi and Winant, Karim Murji and John Solomos link racial formation to racialization, which refers to the "processes by which ideas about race are constructed, come to be regarded as meaningful, and are acted upon" (1).

Racialization therefore assumes that racial categories are not essential but socially and communicatively created. In recognizing affinities and differences between past and present struggles, the identification of racializing processes in genealogy discourses is vital. However, echoing the concerns of critical race theorists such as Derrick Bell, Eric King Watts warns that such antiessentialist notions of race are problematic: "Treating 'race' as merely a social construction misses a crucial facet of its nature. . . . Tropes of 'race' do indeed have a signification system that is textual and material—coded into the institutions we inhabit and the social relations regulated by them" (217–18). Nonetheless, it is possible to negotiate a middle ground between these perspectives by allowing that while signification systems *are* constructed, they still produce material effects in that the racial hierarchies that they create are entrenched in law and other structures of society.

CLAN BY CLAN

While the immigration frame in family history television is present on other genealogy profile series, it is emblematic on *Faces of America* (2010). Gates's opening narration for the second episode endorses the American (Immigrant) Dream in the past tense of postracial, postclass orientations: "America's prosperity depended upon the newcomers' willingness to make sacrifices and work long hours in difficult occupations, yet they often faced discrimination and even outright hostility once they got here."

Profiled on these series are guests of Jewish, Eastern European ancestry whose close kin escaped the Nazi regime, such as Alan Dershowitz (*Finding Your Roots*, 2014), filmmaker Mike Nichols (*Faces of America*), and talk-show host Jerry Springer (*Who Do You Think You Are?*, BBC, 2008). The Holocaust is typically evoked by uncovering the tragic fates of distant family members who stayed behind and/or by pilgrimages to memorial sites. Collective memory studies identify Holocaust and other memorials as loci for public memory in that memorials fix the meanings of memories later circulated by the media (see Wachtel; Young). Visits to such memorials occur in the *Who Do You Think You Are?* profiles of Springer and actors Rashida Jones (NBC, 2012) and Lisa Kudrow (NBC, 2010). In response to Kudrow's segment, a poster on Television without Pity wrote, "I was incredibly moved at the moment where she was standing at the burial pit memorial. The researcher was describing how the events of that day happened, and all Lisa Kudrow could say was 'Oh,' over and over again." Such insertions into a historical moment are common, but if they remain in the moment without the consideration of other histories or present circumstances, there can be no shift to recognizing the plight of others.

On *Finding Your Roots*, the forebears of Rabbi Angela Buchdahl, journalist/talk-show host Barbara Walters, actors Maggie Gyllenhaal and Robert Downey Jr. (2012), Carole King, Tony Kushner, and Alan Dershowitz (2014) are shown to have fled persecution, pogroms, and/or Soviet hegemony. However, beyond revealing that immigrant relatives changed their names because of the anti-Semitism they initially encountered in their new homeland, family history TV has depicted Jewish immigrant life in the United States as upwardly mobile and ultimately postracially hospitable.

On *Who Do You Think You Are?* (NBC), the episodes featuring Martin Sheen (2012) and actor/comedian Rosie O'Donnell (2011) display facets of the Irish Century of Immigration story. However, talk-show host/satirist Stephen Colbert's *Faces of America* profile is more penetrating. Gates explains that one legacy of British colonialism was that persecuted Irish Catholics feared keeping records. He explains the 1840s potato famine and remarks that food was loaded on to ships for export "right in front of the faces of starving people." Colbert proclaims that the resulting exodus "helped the British shipping business," to which Gates adds that the ships took only entire families.

Gates reveals that Colbert's 2X great-grandmother arrived during the 1863 draft riots, during which working-class Irish protested the Civil War draft, having been told that freed slaves would take their jobs. To this, Colbert quips, "And if we don't build a wall between here and Mexico, they're going to take *all* the jobs." Colbert admits that the Irish were indoctrinated not to "fight for black people," grasping a key strategy for inculcating white privilege and allowing his identification to stray momentarily from Irish immigrants to those whose situation was worse. He views anti-Irish cartoons and draws another parallel, seeming to foreshadow Lin-Manuel Miranda's "Yorktown" lyrics from *Hamilton* (2015), which assert immigrants' industriousness and hard work. In noting that his ancestors helped dig the Erie Canal, Colbert maintains that to do this sort of work, "we don't have bulldozers, we have immigrants . . . we still do." Despite his satirical facility for connecting these dots, postidentity sentiment peeks through when Gates asks Colbert what it means to be American: "It's the greatest country in the world, and I could intellectually deconstruct that idea, but I have zero desire to do so." He also marvels that only in America would he marry a woman descended from the English, precisely the people he was raised to revile and feigns shock and displeasure at learning that one of his lineages leads to . . . Lutherans.

Later in the Century of Immigration, Italians arrived en masse, but as of 2017, the quintessential Italian American story remained untold on family history TV. Most of the participants in the mass migration from Italy in the late nineteenth and early twentieth centuries came from its eight southern-most regions, an area referred to as the Mezzogiorno (literally "midday"). According to Nelson Moe, the Mezzogiorno historically has been dismissed, subjugated, impoverished, and hegemonically Othered by the North; the racial implications of its proximity to the Middle East and North Africa facilitate such disregard. In 1983, when Moe was studying in northern Italy, he "decided to go south for the Easter break. When I told the Florentine woman in my compartment that I planned to stop in Naples, a look of dismay spread across her face. Didn't I know that this was a filthy, dangerous city, full of hucksters and thieves? Didn't I know that the south was like Africa? With so many beautiful cities to see in the north, why was I heading to the *Mezzogiorno?*" (locations 46–50). Lest we believe that dismissive, prejudicial attitudes regarding the Mezzogiorno are fully relegated to the past, "Le Mappe degli Stereotipi Europei" (Maps of European Stereotypes), a satirical piece credited to Yanko Tsvetkov and posted by an Italian blogger calling him-self L'Oltreuomo (Overman), redraws maps of Europe with nations labeled according to the stereotypes held by residents of various parts of Europe: Italians identify northern Italy as "Italy" and southern Italy as "Ethiopia."

The movement to unify Italy, the Risorgimento (Resurgence), reached its height in 1860, when military leader Giuseppe Garibaldi "liberated" southern Italy from more than two centuries of Bourbon rule. However, insurrections subsequently flared up within this former Kingdom of the Two Sicilies, sup-ported by the ousted Bourbon king, Francesco (Francis) II, and the Vatican, which feared being swallowed up by a unified Italy with Rome as its capital.

Those in power lumped together the various groups of southern agitators and dismissed them all as brigands or bandits.

By 1870, government troops had quashed these rebellions, and as Jerre Mangione and Ben Morreale observe, "The desperate antagonism of the southerners against their new authorities inevitably gave rise to the speculation that Italy had become a nation in name only. Reflecting on the traumas and ironies attending its beginnings, an Italian statesman in 1870 cautioned that 'although we have made Italy, we have yet to make Italians'" (32). Moe writes that unification "split the nation in two, accentuating the northernness of one part and the southernness of the other" (locations 89–91). In any case, changes wrought by unification did not accrue to the benefit of the burgeoning populations of *contadini* and other rural peasants. On the contrary, the diaspora arose in part as a consequence of worsening poverty, exploitation, and overpopulation resulting from lowered infant mortality rates—a constellation of woes that southern Italians referred to as *la miseria* (the misery). Only this time, the suffering occurred under the auspices of a national government, the Kingdom of Italy led by Vittorio Emanuele (Victor Emmanuel) II, headquartered to the north and administered most visibly by elite figures from northern regions.

Under Bourbon rule, my 3X great-grandfather, a southern landowner, was imprisoned for giving shelter to nationalist troops. According to his hometown (*comune*) website, which lists him as a notable figure, he was arrested and tortured, and although he was later released, his ordeal ultimately led to his death.

The history of the Risorgimento and its consequences for both north and the south remain a matter of strenuous academic debate in Italy. In a recent book, *Terroni* (Dirtballs, a derogatory term used by northerners to denounce southerners), Pino Aprile reports on the atrocities against southerners that took place around the time of the uprisings, which he characterizes as justifiable pushback against northern colonization. According to Aprile, not only do the atrocities remain unacknowledged and uncommemorated, but economic subordination of the south is a continuing legacy of unification. Whereas Naples, the capital of the southern kingdom, was prosperous and productive before unification, Aprile argues, the north was nearing bankruptcy, and southern resources were subsequently plundered to the northern regions' advantage through regressive taxation inordinately affecting the poorer, racialized southerners. Aprile expressly links the history of unification and its resulting inequities to the "induced or forced" mass emigration of southerners (8).

Lorenzo Del Boca responded to Aprile's book with *Polentoni* (Polenta Eaters, a pejorative term for northerners), in which Del Boca endeavors to invalidate ongoing disaffection with Italian unification and justify the anti-immigration stances of Italian leaders whom Aprile expressly denounces as racist. Still, Del Boca acknowledges that the era of unification, including and especially its treatment of southerners, was "a shameful page in history" (back cover).

Gaining a new depth of understanding of the injustices suffered by my ancestors has been an illuminating journey and could have a similar effect on other Italian Americans and Americans in general. The southern tour guide who in 2014 squired my sister and me around the Calabrian village in which our paternal grandmother, Genevieve, was born and then lunched with us at a restaurant in the city of Cosenza confirmed that southern landowners anticipated increasing wealth because of the Risorgimento but in the end were mostly dissatisfied. (My great-grandfather's family eventually vacated its land.) The guide's assertion that Calabrians' welcoming attitude resulted from the fact that northerners seldom visited because they viewed southern-ers as Mafia points to lingering anxieties and divergent interpretations of history and the status quo. In any case, while I do not know precisely why my ancestor backed unification, he did efficiently transmit class privilege to his son, who then ousted his son—my great-grandfather, Francesco—from the family for marrying a poor *contadina*.

Faces of America turns to the half-Italian chef Mario Batali to represent the Italian American experience. Batali's great-grandparents are located on a ship's manifest courtesy of Ancestry.com. They atypically settled in the American West, where hardships in the mines ensued. Gates helps make Grandmother Batali's oxtail ravioli and shares dinner with several genera-tions of the chef's family. Batali mentions two ancestral towns in the north-central region of Tuscany and another in Abruzzo, which is a region of the Mezzogiorno. However, the racialization, economic exploitation, and inequitable impact of Italian unification that uprooted countless southern Italians escapes notice. Seemingly unaware of this history, Batali wonders why anyone left the "idyllic world of Italy," where, he contends, few were in need. To this, Gates offers no pushback.

Footage of Batali in Italy that appeared in a promotional spot for the program apparently left on the cutting room floor might have filled in some of these blanks, but especially juxtaposed with the Irish immigrant story depicted in Colbert's segments of *Faces of America*, Batali's piece was disap-pointing, revealing significant flaws in the criteria used for casting these programs. Batali's ethnic visibility as a chef of Italian cuisines does not mean that his family history epitomizes the Italian immigrant experience in a way that opens up teachable moments in an immigration-themed show. While many educated Americans can link Irish immigration to the potato famine and even to British colonialism and Eastern European Jewish immigration to anti-Semitic persecution, specifics regarding the history and context of Italian immigration beyond some generalized perception of poverty are unfamiliar to most Americans—including, it would seem, the program's creators and some celebrated Italian Americans. Thus, the show paints a postclass, postracial picture, and a key opportunity to educate on this matter and draw parallels with the causes and effects of immigration today is missed. Indeed, according to David Leonhardt, the economic, linguistic, and educational trajectories of today's Latina/o immigrants are most reminiscent of the Italian immigrants who arrived in the late nineteenth and early twentieth centuries.

On the PBS website for *Faces of America*, Italians and Italian Americans remarked about the lack of historical context in the Batali profile. One commenter wrote, "My main reason for replying here is to ask those who still have no answer for 'Why They Came' to research the history of Italy during your ancestor's immigration years. I think that journey would be extremely rewarding and eye opening as you peel away the romantic onion. . . . Read European and Italian history, especial[l]y for the South of Italy, starting in the mid 1800's." Another participant reacted with a *me-too-ist* bent: "The Batali portrait is by and large a wash and doesn't fully reflect the experience and sufferings of Italians in America. . . . Many other profiles admit discrimination and yet this is largely left out where it pertains to olive skin."

This comment brought to my mind situations from my childhood that were beyond my comprehension at the time. In the postwar era, working-class first- and second-generation Americans whose ancestors migrated from Eastern and Southern Europe were among those able to capitalize on the class mobility afforded by the GI Bill. However, they still stuck out like sore thumbs in many persistently WASP-ish suburbs, such as ours outside Washington, DC. There, a disagreement erupted between my father and a fellow World War II veteran who lived in the house on the corner. His children were our playmates until the man, who had lost a leg in the war, bellowed "Dirty Dago" at my father. On another occasion, the most popular girl at school informed me that she would not invite me to her birthday party because I was Catholic and consequently "not a Christian." My mother had a confrontation with my public school kindergarten teacher after the teacher asked parents to send hangers to school for use in the classroom coat closet. At my mother's suggestion, I brought a pink, satin-covered, plush hanger handcrafted by my grandmother, primarily because it would make my coat easier to spot. However, every morning, the teacher held the hanger aside and gave it to another student as she entered. My mother, who taught kindergarten at a different public school, took a day off from work and walked me to school to address the situation. A few years later, my mother explained to me that the teacher "didn't like where our family came from," leaving me to wonder what was so wrong with New York.

Most of these occurrences might be classified as little more than micro-aggressions, but they were vestiges of structural, discriminatory treatment faced by my immigrant forebears. As chronicled by a 2015 PBS documentary miniseries, *The Italian Americans*, Irish American control of the US Roman Catholic Church relegated Italian newcomers to second-class status. In the early twentieth century, many churches forced Italians to attend Mass in basement chapels because Irish clergy and parishioners considered Italian reverence for patron saints and their sculptural representations to be the worship of false idols.

I frequently overheard family chatter about Irish-Italian conflicts within the Church as I grew up and witnessed remnants of it after transferring to parochial school. My internalization of inferiority in this regard became evident when an incident occurred while I was visiting my grandparents in Queens. At my grandmother's recommendation, I went to Confession after Sunday Mass as she did, only to receive a tongue-lashing in Irish brogue from the priest, who was livid because parish children were restricted from making confession at that time. I was only seven and so intimidated that I could not muster enough volume to explain that I was only visiting.

The Italian Americans resonates in other ways. According to family lore, the surname of my paternal grandfather and his siblings was unceremoniously altered from *Scuteri* to *Scodari* by faculty at their Irish-controlled parochial school, much as the documentary illustrates via the example of celebrated educator Leonard Covello, whose original surname was changed by a teacher who thought *Coviello* was too difficult to pronounce. According to the hosts of *Genealogy Roadshow* (PBS, 2016), in contrast to popular belief, the carefully selected officials at Ellis Island seldom misreported the names of incoming migrants.

The Italian Americans also notes that southern Italian immigrants experienced discrimination in terms of both mortgage redlining schemes and racial designations on official forms. The "South Italian" and "Latin" racial categorizations appeared on many of the documents I encountered, indicating that the popular belief of northern Italians that those from the Mezzogiorno were racially suspect was for a time reproduced on American shores. However, this topic has received little discussion on family history TV.

To combat stereotypes, one person of Italian descent on the PBS discussion board for *Faces of America*'s Batali profile hegemonically reproduced those clichés in response to the reference to the "olive skin" of Italian Americans. The ensuing exchange reenacted divisions between northern and southern Italians along colorist lines while demonstrating a dearth of knowledge concerning the specific contours of the Italian diaspora: "I am 100% ITALIAN, and my entire family is blond haired (strawberry blonde) with green or hazel eyes. We are from Northern [I]taly. . . . The dark olive skinned TV stereotype is more common in southern [I]taly where it is more rural, uneducated and where the Mafia was born." One of several counter-arguments got quickly to the point: "I'm 100% Italian as well and I'm olive skinned with dark hair and eyes. Simply because someone made an erroneous assumption about what Italians should look like doesn't give you the right to imply that if you look stereotypically Italian and are from central or southern Italy you're stupid and a criminal."

On *Who Do You Think You Are?*, three Italian Americans with known roots in the Mezzogiorno—actors Steve Buscemi (2011), Edie Falco (2012), and Ashley Judd (2011)—follow a non-Italian lineage. Visiting ancestral spots in *central and northern* Italy are four Italian Americans—actors Marisa Tomei (2013), Valerie Bertinelli (2015), Brooke Shields (2010), and Susan Sarandon (2010). Sarandon also has *southern* Italian roots that remain unexplored. *Finding Your Roots* fares a bit better in profiling chef Tom Colicchio (2014) and comic/talk-show host Jimmy Kimmel (2016), superficially citing their southern heritage without scrutinizing it in terms of the unification of Italy in the mid-1800s or the racialized, subaltern status of southerners. These programs also appear to avoid travel to southern Italy. The Colicchio profile alludes to racism against Italians in the United States but, in general, the programs reflect a northern Italian bias, replicating but never elucidating a major, racially tinged dividing line that helped cause the Italian diaspora.

Stereotypes remain in play in terms of Middle Eastern and Muslim heritage. *Faces of America* profiles Jordan's Queen Noor, who was born in the United States as Lisa Halaby and was the great-granddaughter of one of the first Syrian immigrants to the United States. Halaby converted to Islam when she married Jordan's King Hussein. In telling Noor's story, Gates explains that for decades, the United States permitted only whites to naturalize, a critical piece of information that is mostly ignored elsewhere in *Faces of America* and other genealogy TV texts. Middle Easterners lobbied to be considered white, touting the Christianity some of them professed. Gates is shocked at good press the Halaby family received and jokes, "The Irish were demeaned in the press." Noor's sharp-witted rejoinder, "Like we are now," is mindful of racialization's fickle character. This exchange shows how any supposed assimilation is not irreversible; targeted racializing discourses can always emerge or reemerge.

Other profiles feature more recent migrations. *Faces of America* features doctor and talk-show host Mehmet Oz, whose parents migrated to the United States from Turkey, where there is uneasy separation of church and state. He explains that his mother was raised a secular Muslim while his father was more conservative and that Christians have a similar division in the United States. Oz professes affinity for separation of church and state and the "spiritual" rather than "legal" aspects of Islam in the style of the mystical Sufis.

On *Finding Your Roots* (2012), we learn that conservative imam Yasir Qadhi's moderately Muslim Pakistani family emigrated for economic reasons and that he was educated and sensitized after 9/11, retracting his previous denial of the Holocaust. To punctuate this reversal, he is shown with Gates at the 9/11 Memorial in New York, pointing out Muslim names among the victims. For both Qadhi and Sanjay Gupta (*Finding Your Roots*, 2012), Gates narrates that the 1947 partition of India created Pakistan as a separate Muslim state and that mass relocations and violence ensued. Gupta's Hindu family was uprooted as Qadhi's left for Pakistan. However, only Qadhi's profile explicitly ties the upheaval to British colonial rule.

In chronicling the journeys of East Asians, *Finding Your Roots* (2012) pinpoints Margaret Cho's fractured identity as the American child of Korean newcomers. However, the *Faces of America* profile of cellist Yo-Yo Ma, a musical prodigy born in Paris to expatriate Chinese, and the *Who Do You Think You Are?* profile of journalist/talk-show host Julie Chen, whose parents emigrated from China as students, conveniently bypass periods in which immigration exclusions were aimed at this group.

Genealogy TV's depiction of Latina/os, especially in regard to immigration, is crucial. An episode of *Finding Your Roots* (2012) brings together actors Michelle Rodriguez and Adrian Grenier with conservative political commentator Linda Chavez, and a profile on *Faces of America* centers on actor Eva Longoria. All of these individuals have deep roots on what is currently US territory—Rodriguez via her Puerto Rican father, and the others via the longtime Mexican presence in the American Southwest. Rodriguez recalls living with her maternal grandmother, a Dominican immigrant to the United States. However, according to the narrative, the only version of "immigration" shared by the four is that of Spanish invaders and colonizers who initially mixed with indigenous peoples. Later, some of their family trees grew tangled branches of "consanguinity," or the intermarriage of cousins to dilute any non-European in the bloodline.

Exploration of documents confirms that Chavez is descended from Sephardic "crypto-Jews" who pretended to convert during the Spanish Inquisition. The episode displays horrific drawings of this chapter in history to viewers. While some in the audience *might* stop to think that a number of faiths have given rise to violent religious extremism at various times in history and that such occasions have not resulted in condemnation of the entire faith in perpetuity, the text in no way encourages this thinking or the contemporary parallels it might expose. Elsewhere, *Who Do You Think You Are?* (2015) mentions in passing the immigration of actor America Ferrera's Honduran parents but highlights the history of her great-grandfather, a revolutionary. In any case, while it is critical to show that many Mexican Americans have longer claims to US territory than do most whites, these series do not feature recent or recollected arrivals from Latin America or many other places or touch on recent immigration debates. The programs address neither the fluid, variously motivated, racist and racializing rhetoric regarding Latina/os and others nor the burgeoning anti-immigrant zeal.

A 2014 episode of *Finding Your Roots* (2014) exploring the family histories of chefs Ming Tsai, Aarón Sánchez, and Tom Colicchio might have plugged some of these holes in the immigration stories of Chinese, Mexican, and Italian Americans. However, the episode neglects to mention the Chinese Exclusion Act, which remained in force until after China entered World War II against Japan and a Chinese communist takeover loomed—the events that brought Ming Tsai's ancestors to US shores. The episode also bypasses the immigration story of Sánchez's mother, who grew up on the family ranch in Mexico, in favor of that of a more distant forebear who left the ranch and fled across the border during the Mexican Revolution of 1910–20. He later returned to Mexico and reestablished the ranch, and the episode again sidesteps recent controversies involving immigration from Mexico and elsewhere in Latin America. Moreover, after Gates traces an ancestral line back to Spain and asks how Sánchez will answer when his children wonder about their heritage, he responds, "Mexican American by way of Basque country, Spain," as if all the family's lineages passed through Europe. Finally, the episode mentions that Colicchio's paternal family origins are located in Campania, in southern Italy, but does not explain the Risorgimento or contextualize the hardships his ancestors suffered that motivated their eventual departure. A distant uncle who was executed as a brigand is simply assumed to have been no more than a reprobate without political motives.

Avoidance of immigration controversies and the true history of the Italian diaspora continues during the 2016 season of *Finding Your Roots*. The profile of Chinese American architect Maya Lin allows the Chinese Exclusion Act to remain unacknowledged, as it was no longer in force when her forebears arrived. The profile of actor/singer Lea Michele acknowledges her mother's Italian heritage but explores her father's Sephardic Jewish background. *Finding Your Roots* also profiles yet another Italian American chef, Lidia Bastianich, who comes from a diasporic background that is atypical of Italian Americans in the United States. Bastianich was born in Istria, a sliver of northern Italy that became part of Yugoslavia after World War II. Her ethnic Italian family was oppressed by the new regime and escaped into Italy, eventually migrating to the United States. PBS's 2015 documentary miniseries, *The Italian Americans*, links the Italian diaspora to the history of the Risorgimento but does not acknowledge the related and still smoldering controversies. Today's Italy is, after all, the same Italy that was created by unification, and anything that might appear to besmirch its historical integrity is seemingly a taboo subject on genealogy TV.

The introduction of host Mary Tedesco, a half Italian American specialist in Italian genealogy, in the second season of *Genealogy Roadshow* (2015), has not provided a fuller picture. In one segment, she travels to Sicily in the hopes of linking an Italian American family's heritage to a noble crest—the only visit to southern Italy of a host or guest on any of the US family history television programs analyzed here. On *Finding Your Roots* (2014), three Greek Americans—comic actor/writer Tina Fey, journalist and former White House aide George Stephanopoulos, and writer David Sedaris—absorb a more penetrating history of what spurred their ancestors' immigration even though far greater numbers of Italian Americans arrived in the United States.

While *Faces of America* elevates immigration and the American mosaic but fails to address recent controversies, a poster on a *Wall Street Journal* blog responding to an article by Jeffrey Podolsky on the use of genetic ancestry in *Faces of America* was peeved that the program's immigrant content did not highlight earlier immigrant histories. This poster hegemonically implied that the English and Scottish are somehow marginalized groups in terms of American history and family history discourses: "While the stories of those featured are fascinating, it is disingenuous of Gates to have completely omitted the English (and Scots) who were integral to the settling of North

America and overwhelmingly responsible for founding the United States of America, thus providing all later immigrants a free and welcoming country. Shame on you Professor Gates for your reverse racism and revisionist agenda." From the opposite perspective, a poster on Television without Pity became annoyed with *Who Do You Think You Are?* (NBC, 2010) when actor Sarah Jessica Parker responded to the information that her American lineage led back to colonial times by "going on and on about how she felt so much more American and she didn't really feel like a real American before, but now all of a sudden she's legit—kind of goes against the whole 'American dream' idea and implies immigrants (who weren't original colonists) are less 'American.'" However, a second Television without Pity user expressed the importance of learning about his/her family's immigrant experiences to "connect" to historical knowledge.

One commentator on Television without Pity suggested in response to the US adaptation of *Who Do You Think You Are?* (2010) that audiences might be turned off when these series venture beyond pure escapism and attempt to make meaningful connections to historical struggles: "The original (British) series is actually really good, very moving and serious. They mostly featured legit respected actors with a genuine interest in their family history, and the celeb element was downplayed. It could be far too emotionally manipulative in the, [']here's an actor crying over hearing the details of their great grand-mother dying in the Holocaust/grandfather dying in the potato famine' way though." This post resistively disapproves of the celebrity-centered narratives while hegemonically privileging "legit" actors. It also displays a hegemonic disinclination to collective imagination in terms of wanting to illuminate difficult histories and, by implication, their contemporary correlates, whether or not the text gestures toward such associations.

The analyses of genealogy television have thus far exposed biases related to race and/or ethnicity, often intersecting with gender and/or class, in genealogical documents, practices, and television representations. Auto-ethnographic insights and other data reinforce the idea that genealogical documents and relevant cultural practices often manifest preexisting class and gender biases that can affect the performance, meaning, and implications of genealogy. Moreover, family history television texts are steeped in patriarchy and post- orientations. They carry the postidentity cachets of celebrities—particularly women, who are vehicles of postfeminist consumerism as they model designer labels. These texts reproduce the white savior trope of inferential racism and/or endorse solutions based in individual, not collective, empowerment.

Even the mockumentary series *Family Tree* (HBO, 2013) with its satirical gibes that gesture in the direction of multicultural fetishization and other excesses of the family history television genre, does not deliver an appreciable, coherent critique. Indeed, audiences on the surveyed sites do not appear to respond to the program as a critique of anything specific to genealogy. To many such respondents, genealogy is merely the vehicle to ignite a whimsical, offbeat narrative that could as easily exist through other mechanisms.

Genealogy TV narratives reflect the fact that economic exploitation, oppression, and/or racism have spurred migration to the United States from many lands. However, a number of immigrant groups—for instance, immigrants from African nations—have not as of 2017 had their stories told on these programs. In addition, these narratives occasionally paint incomplete, decontextualized, and one-sided pictures of the motivations for flight. Seldom are these stories linked to the present to prompt counterhegemonic associations with and divergences from ongoing struggles. On *Faces of America*, Queen Noor alludes to the fact that even though her family supposedly assimilated after arriving in the United States, bigotry against Middle Easterners (who are often assumed to all be Muslims) is now resurgent. But the underlying principle at work is neither fully articulated nor expanded.

Despite a long history of prejudice, Mexican Americans and other Latina/os were classified as white by the Census Bureau until the late twentieth century (see Passel). Unlike African and Asian American citizens, Latinos fought alongside whites in World War II. Still today, the terms *Hispanic* and *Latina/o* indicate a minority culture in the United States with a history of discrimination against it, defined according to Latin American nationality, origin, and/or diaspora; Spanish language; and a mixture of Spanish, indigenous American, and sometimes African racial attributes. Outside this very specific orientation, however, this is arguably racial hybridity. According to Carlos Lozada, "If all ethnic identities are created, imagined or negotiated to some degree, American Hispanics provide an especially stark example." Pope Francis, recognized as the first Latino pope based on his native Spanish language and Argentinian birth and citizenship, has two ethnically Italian parents. In addition, Spanish celebrities such as Antonio Banderas and Penélope Cruz with no background or experience of diaspora or mixed racial identity associated with Latin America, are often categorized as Latina/o or Hispanic.

These designations are even less clear outside the Americas, as ambiguity born of hybridity exists everywhere. Dominican American Raquel Cepeda's memoir, *Bird of Paradise*, chronicles her journey to "become Latina" in part by noting how her race/ethnicity reads in various parts of the world: "In Europe, people have mistaken me for Andalusian, Turkish, Brazilian, and North African. In North and West Africa, I've been asked if I'm of Arabic or Amazigh [Berber] descent. In New York, Los Angeles, and Miami, it varies: Israeli or Sephardic, Palestinian, Moroccan, biracial Black and white American, Brazilian, and so on. I've been mistaken for being everything except what I am: Dominican" (locations 88–93).

In the American and particularly the US context, the process of Latinidad, or "being, becoming, and/or performing belonging within the Latina/o diaspora" (Valdivia locations 1263–65) as well as a recognition of continuing nativist and racially exclusionary rhetoric and policies directed at Latina/os have racialized the category in common understandings. Sociologist Marta Tienda concurs that Latina/os have "become a race by default, just by usage of the category" (qtd. in Lozado). The AncestryDNA ad in which a woman identifying as Hispanic as if it is a single "race" is surprised to learn that she is "everything" based on the various geographic affinities indicated on her DNA pie chart. The point here is not to minimize the significance of *Latina/o* as designating a group connected by language, geography, diaspora and most significantly a history of specifically and racially contextualized discriminatory treatment. Rather, this example illuminates the mechanisms of racialization, including in texts of family history.

The fact that much immigration was legal during the Century of Immigration did not prevent nativism from flaring up, thereby leading to draconian restrictions. By pointedly explaining the 1924 cutoff for the Century of Immigration and noting the ebb and flow of ostensibly racial categories, genealogy series might have also shed light on the constructedness of race and hinted that when it comes to today's immigrants, evoking the absence of documentation is a rationalization. Despite Colbert's quick-witted associations between Irish immigrants and today's newcomers, family history television neglects current controversies and affirms postracial, postclass, and postfeminist orientations.

In June 2011, I stood at the (doubly metaphorical) bottom of Italy's boot, in my paternal ancestral town of Roccella Ionica, Reggio Calabria, Calabria, and gazed out on the Ionian Sea, an arm of the Mediterranean. From there, Greece and Turkey were to my left, Tunisia was to my right, Libya was in front of me, and Europe was behind. I was instantly aware that this place was at a crossroads of three continents and that its history played a role in producing me. However, the knack for filling in the blanks and relating such insights to current politics is not assured. To the extent I manage to do it, it is because of the cultural competencies of my profession. For family history television and other media to effectively educate, sensitize, and mobilize, however, the concerns of the present must be recognized more pointedly and plainly in the trials of the past.

TUBULAR GENEALOGY III

Identity and Genetic Ancestry in Genealogy Television and
Related Texts and Practices

(COLOR-)BLINDED BY SCIENCE

According to Barbara A. Koenig, Sandra Soo-Jin Lee, and Sarah S. Richardson, when the international Human Genome Project finished mapping the human genome in 2003, one of its key findings was that all human DNA is 99.9 percent identical, with only 3 percent of what remains linking individuals to the human migration patterns that inform genetic ancestry (1). The authors go on to emphasize that the vast majority of social scientists, medical ethicists, geneticists, and other scientists concur that geographic genetic markers are not the equivalent of racial categories; on the contrary, racial categories are not evident in DNA but, rather, are socially constructed. However, this view can be contentious. Eric King Watts expresses concern that by discussing race purely as a social construction, we may overlook its material effects, which are "coded into the institutions we inhabit and the social relations regulated by them" (217–18). Actor Don Cheadle alludes to this idea on *African American Lives 2* (2008), when he explains how he navigates mixed racial identity: "You are what you have to defend."

The assertion of racial social construction should not be accepted as a blanket disclaimer. Even if signification systems, including race, are constructed, they have real-world impact. Indeed, Koenig, Lee, and Richardson warn that many recent genetic studies have "revived the idea of racial categories as proxies for biological differences" (1). In gauging the possibilities for a critical genealogy—and precisely because of the materiality of inequitable and unjust outcomes—it is crucial to ask whether racial categories are being newly constructed, reconstructed, reinforced, and/or challenged by institutions, texts, and/or practices of genetic ancestry. We might also ask whether representations and realizations of racial/ethnic hybridity associated with genetic ancestry break down essentialist notions of race with counterhegemonic results. It is also appropriate to consider the extent to which a focus on genetic heritage deemphasizes or obscures alternative definitions of family and other cultural forms of connectedness or relations of power.

Firms marketing genetic ancestry (or genetic genealogy) testing services—AncestryDNA, African Ancestry, AfricanDNA, Family Tree DNA, and 23andMe, among others—have proliferated since the Human Genome Project completed its work. In 2006, Henry T. Greely counted fifteen companies plus the National Geographic Society's Genographic Project that provided such services, and this number has continued to increase. The earliest protocols for genetic ancestry testing primarily involved *mitochondrial DNA* (mtDNA), found in both men and women but passed on only by mothers, and *Y chromosome DNA* (Y-DNA), found only in men and passed from father to son. Each tests the deep (distant) ancestry reflected in one lineage, whether the direct maternal line (mtDNA) or the direct paternal line (Y-DNA). Women interested in exploring their patrilineal genetic ancestry must acquire results from a second DNA test performed on their father or another male descended from the same paternal line, often at additional expense. Questions arise regarding whether and how these companies and genealogy-related texts represent this science and explain its significance and whether DNA firms market their testing kits at the same cost to both men and women regardless of the number of tests performed. An intersected gender element consequently enters into our assessment of the ethnic and racial implications of genetic ancestry services and discourses.

Since mtDNA and Y-DNA do not undergo recombination of paternal and maternal genetic material with each iteration of the family tree, their mutations or markers, which are generated at rare intervals of up to thousands of years, are evidence of a person's descent from ancient, migratory populations referred to as *haplogroups*. Haplogroups spring into existence when a specific genetic mutation is shown to have occurred, which then helps characterize the group. An mtDNA or Y-DNA haplogroup can indicate a genetic vintage, a line of descent, and a migratory route. However, an mtDNA or Y-DNA haplogroup to which one belongs represents only one of a person's multitudinous lineages. Surname matching often accompanies Y-DNA studies, underscoring the masculine emphasis of such efforts. In fact,

Debbie Kennett notes that genetic genealogists use term *daughtering out* to describe when a Y-DNA lineage and accompanying surname reach a dead end because only daughters remain (locations 858–63).

To supplement information drawn from the paternal and maternal lineages, however, *autosomal* or *admixture* tests, often referred to in marketing as *ethnic ancestry* tests, examine an array of mutations from *throughout* the genome. Testing for these *ancestry informative markers* (AIMS) has become prevalent and compares the AIMS of the subject to those of other subjects from various geographic populations. Most firms initially identified these groups more or less continentally—that is, by African, European, Asian, and Native American designations—but the determination of subcategories eventually became possible. However, the ability to demonstrate a genetic relationship to a particular population is only as good as the degree to which the testing service has collected samples within that population.

Problematically, continental designations, whether subdivided or not, tend to coincide with culturally constructed racial classifications. Greely notes that geographic markers can be used interchangeably with racial categories as a kind of shorthand. Doing so, however, provides grist for racist, racializing rhetoric. As Andrew Smart, Richard Tutton, Paul Martin, and George T. H. Ellison argue, "Racialization is not simply a 'problematic outcome' of biomedical science but also appears to play a significant role in shaping the very contours of the subject which scientists are struggling to better comprehend" (49). David Mountain and Jeanne Guelke concur that the "current diversity of geographic backgrounds and political ideologies of deep genealogists will problematize the issue of racial identities" (158).

The article "Race and Science" linked to PBS's web page for *African American Lives* (2006) situates the genetic ancestry significance of migratory populations and other genetic informants of ethnicity in relation to popular conceptions of race but preserves the notion of racial categories as social constructions: "Over time, these groups of migratory humans became isolated from one another, and eventually mutation and other evolutionary pressures produced slight genetic changes, some of which are responsible for the differences in appearance we've commonly used to divide up human beings into racial groups." This explication of genetic ancestry makes an appropriately nuanced distinction between migratory populations and constructed racial categories without pretending that associations between them are unlikely to surface. However, the research narratives in genealogy texts tend to allow ethnic ancestry classifications to stand in for racial ones.

TELEVISION, GENETIC ANCESTRY, AND IDENTITY

The Big C: Hereafter (Showtime, 2013) contains the final chapters of *The Big C* (Showtime, 2010–12), a drama series chronicling the life and death of Cathy Jamison (Laura Linney), a mother, wife, and high school history teacher stricken with terminal melanoma (skin cancer). As these final chapters commence, Cathy has learned that her remission is over and that she is in irreversible decline. At school, she no longer has patience for protocol and red tape. When she pays for her students' genetic ancestry tests, her principal confronts her, declaring, "It's not history." She replies, "Turns out two of my white kids are blacker than my black kid. If you think that didn't provoke interesting conversation, you'd be wrong."

Despite the potential for using hybridity in genetic ancestry as a mechanism for insight, as Cathy does, or for equating genetic ancestry designations with culturally constructed racial categories, as Cathy also does, DNA in many cases supplies the only means by which the descendants of African slaves can make a connection to African geographic locations and peoples. These subjects' DNA markers can be matched to those of contemporary Africans. As seen most clearly in *Faces of America* (2010), where African American school kids are linked to African tribes, such potential for empowerment drives much (but definitely not all) use of genetic ancestry on family history TV. Mountain and Guelke also tout the "subversive potential" of genetic ancestry, based on the case in which DNA vindicated a group of African Americans claiming descent from Thomas Jefferson and one of his slaves, Sally Hemings.

The first episodes of both *African American Lives* and *African American Lives 2* situate the special case of African Americans. Gates introduces the first series from Ellis Island, reminding viewers that some Americans cannot trace their ancestry through there, and hints at new avenues available for such searches. The final episode of each series reveals the results of guests' DNA tests, which might aid in efforts to scale their brick walls. In *African American Lives*, we are told that Gates's admixture indicates that he is 50 percent white. Oprah Winfrey has no white ancestry but does possess a smidgen of Native American background. Astronaut Mae Jemison, who assumed that she had Native American origins because of her appearance, instead has East Asian heritage—a product, Gates suggests, of mingling between blacks and Chinese laborers in the United States.

On *African American Lives 2*, Gates's mtDNA suggests European origins along this maternal lineage, which is rare among African Americans. Gates is initially perplexed, much like a viewer who confessed on the show's Television without Pity forum, "I'd always assumed that my ancestors were products of slave rape, and imagine my surprise when that turned out not to be the case at all." In Gates's case, conventional genealogy determined that a white female indentured servant worked alongside and procreated with a male African slave in colonial America.

Following this revelation, *African American Lives 2* acknowledges a DNA link to a white family and conventional research pointing to European—in this case, Irish—ancestry on Gates's paternal line. In Ireland, his Y-DNA verifies his descent from a notorious warlord, King Niall of the Nine Hostages, an inheritance Gates apparently shares with Sergeant James Crowley, the police officer who arrested Gates on 16 July 2009 for breaking into his own home in Cambridge, Massachusetts. The arrest led to a public debate concerning racial profiling that grew to involve President Obama (see Whittington). The show's segment in Ireland follows Gates to a university genetics lab and classroom; to a hillside, where he encounters other Niall descendants; and to a pub, where he guzzles Guinness with his newly discovered compatriots, communicating the bemused but welcoming attitude of both Gates and the Irish folk around him. While the segment suggests that hybridity revealed via DNA can expand horizons, these series should not diminish pressing *cultural* stances such as those held on behalf of the descendants of African slaves, including Gates, for whom "European" DNA *is* often (and likely is in this case) a consequence of kidnapping and rape.

Elsewhere in *African American Lives 2*, Gates shows clear affinity for his African progenitors, prompting a hegemonic response from a viewer on Television without Pity: "What's with this 'our people' crap? Gates is half white! Sorry, but the unfortunate aspect of genealogy is that you have to claim all your ancestors, and not just the ones you feel empathy towards." This sentiment flies in the face of Anne-Marie Kramer's view that "kinship can be both acknowledged *and* disavowed" via genealogical practices ("Kinship" 393). However, another Television without Pity user countered, "I wouldn't call it 'crap.' What people is Gates supposed to identify with, anyway? Being African-American means that you have a mixed racial ancestry (some more than others). When people see him, they see an African American. And, it's all well and good for white people to dictate what ethnicity HLG should claim, but for most of the history of the USA we haven't been able to make that choice."

Gates; comedians Chris Rock, Chris Tucker, and Wanda Sykes; actors Don Cheadle and Morgan Freeman; jazzman Branford Marsalis; and poets

Elizabeth Alexander and Maya Angelou are among the African Americans traced back to African tribes in the PBS celebrity profile series. On *African American Lives 2*, by incorporating DNA information, a historian narrows the number of voyages through the Middle Passage on which Gates's ancestors may have been held captive. On *Who Do You Think You Are?* (NBC, 2012), actor Blair Underwood's admixture is determined and markers are linked to a distant cousin in Africa, prompting a visit there by him and his father. The narrator explains that in 2005, Ancestry.com took African samples to market genetic testing based on matching to African Americans.

On Television without Pity, African Americans appreciated the encouragement to have DNA testing that *African American Lives* provided. One exclaimed: "Loved the show! I would pay for a DNA test to find what 'tribe' I'm from!" Another concurred, "I too am from one of those black families that doesn't talk much about the family past the great grandfather stage and I was totally wanting to gather up all the stories I've heard and have them verified and take my DNA test. So I guess Gates was effective."

Once or twice in the PBS celebrity profile series, Gates warns that providers examine only one lineage when testing mtDNA or Y-DNA. Still, these programs present genetic ancestry without a clear but nuanced explanation similar to the one provided on the PBS web page for *African American Lives*—and with little caution about the racist and racializing misapplications of genetic ancestry. However, these series do reflect the fluidity of what we call race in that the way we might categorize individuals may not fully conform to their genetic makeup.

Not every online respondent to family history television had a benign or counterhegemonic reaction to this prospect. In 2012, a Television without Pity commentator suggested that *Who Do You Think You Are?* was part of an elaborate conspiracy theory:

> Now that NBC managed to get their man into the white house they realize that his support is taking off like rats off a burning ship. Some people would be surprised to know that approx. 10% of whites have some black ancestry that they don't know about. Most of Thomas Jefferson's progeny are of African blood. Is this how NBC will try to persuade us to take Obama back into our loving embrace?

This poster and those who share his/her views perceive that highlighting racial hybridity poses a threat to essentialist notions of racial purity and white privilege, whether in the election of a biracial president, the controversial

2013 Cheerios commercial highlighting a little girl from an interracial family, or revelations of multiracial ancestry on genealogy TV. While Catherine Squires argues that genealogy has the potential to undermine purity narratives, she also states that such results are neither guaranteed "nor the only possibilities that may emerge" (211). One such unanticipated possibility is a reactionary stance that might stick out like a sore thumb on a particular social media site but become conventional wisdom on another.

When it comes to the product placements for genetic ancestry testing services on family history television, the programs interpellate several groups as potential consumers. *Faces of America* and *Finding Your Roots* (2012–) give various genetic ancestry tests by 23andMe and/or Family Tree DNA to guests of many heritages. When Gates reports results to Yasir Qadhi, a conservative imam of Pakistani descent, on *Finding Your Roots* (2012), the host warns that ethnicity and religion do not always correspond. Qadhi's patrilineal haplogroup unsurprisingly goes back to India, but it also associates him with Ashkenazi Jews. At first startled, Qadhi reasons that many observers believe that Jews and Muslims are cousins. Also on *Finding Your Roots* (2012), actor Robert Downey Jr. predicts that he has a bit of African and Native American ancestry, but his admixture is 100 percent European. Gates jokes that Downey's role in the satirical film *Tropic Thunder*, in which he portrayed a white Australian actor playing an African American actor in a film within the film, was really acting after all. On *Faces of America*, tests also determine mtDNA and/or Y-DNA haplogroups but specifically frame those whose family trees indicate mixed racial ancestry as a target market for autosomal "ethnic ancestry" tests.

Faces of America compares the genetic markers of profiled guests, revealing that many pairs share an ancestor within a few centuries: Dr. Mehmet Oz and Mike Nichols, Nichols and actor Meryl Streep, Yo-Yo Ma and Eva Longoria, Queen Noor and Mario Batali, and Stephen Colbert and Elizabeth Alexander. On *Finding Your Roots* (2012), Martha Stewart's mtDNA and standard genealogy connect her to Muslim Tatars, while MtDNA links both Maggie Gyllenhaal and Kyra Sedgwick to the Near East via their mothers' Jewish roots: Gates explains that 40 percent of Eastern European Jews share genetics going back three thousand years to just four women.

Finding Your Roots (2012) highlights Latin American heritage as actors Michelle Rodriguez and Adrian Grenier and political pundit Linda Chavez inspect autosomal results estimating their indigenous ancestry to be under 10 percent—far less than their European ancestry. This finding displeases Grenier and the half-Dominican Rodriguez, who does welcome the 20 percent African in her bloodline. Plugging the testing firms, Gates reveals that Chavez's DNA reflects 20 percent Middle Eastern heritage, likely because she is descended from Sephardic Jews. Similarly, on *Genealogy Roadshow* (2013), genetic testing confirms the similar suspicions held by a young Chicana. On *Faces of America* (2010), Eva Longoria expresses pride in her 27 percent Native American ancestry. She is also 3 percent African, prompting Gates to remind us that Mexico, too, had African slaves. Also on *Faces of America*, writer Louise Erdrich, who is white and Native American, refuses a DNA test that might unsettle her family's cultural identification with the Chippewa. In 2006, a Television without Pity poster described an analogous, counterhegemonic impulse to privilege culture over genetics in response to the use of continental autosomal classifications in the ethnic ancestry percentages presented to guests on *African American Lives*:

> I don't think I would want to know, because, I feel that whatever "percentage" is white or whatever is irrelevant—I am Black because of a culture and a common struggle of my ancestors. I can look around my family and see the yellow and redbone, the noses and the eye colors to tell me that it wasn't a direct trip from Ile de Gor[ée]. I don't need a DNA test to tell me that.

An article by Alondra Nelson and Won Hwang makes a similar point about the preeminence of culture as it examines celebratory YouTube videos in which African Americans reveal the results of DNA tests intended to establish their genetic link to African locations and peoples.

Participants on a blog devoted to Latinas hotly debated Longoria's genetic ancestry in response to an article by Gerri Miller touting Longoria's "surprising roots." They interpreted this characterization to refer to her 3 percent African background in addition to her 70 percent Spanish and 27 percent Native American, which are more common for a mestiza. Although Gates explains on *Faces of America* that Longoria's African ancestry probably resulted from the historical presence of African slaves in Mexico, several discussants on the blog were certain that this DNA must instead be evidence of the Moorish, North African presence in Spain. One participant characterized North Africans as essentially "Caucasian" and consequently distinguishable from African. Others were more frank about their suspicions regarding Longoria's African heritage: "I honestly think it has been tampered with, she doesn't have African DNA." Still others seemed more concerned about the implications of slave ownership than race: "Why the association with slaves if she is related to Africans? There were African settlers in [North America] that were FREE."

The consanguinity of bloodlines created through the racially motivated intermarriage of cousins revealed in *Finding Your Roots*'s profiles of Rodriguez and Chavez provides some corroboration of this resistance to embracing mixed-race heritage among Latina/os. However, Rodriguez specifically welcomes both her indigenous and African roots. Raquel Cepeda's quest to clarify her hybrid identity partly through DNA testing to come to terms with being "Latina" offers another confirmation of a historical preference for whiteness among some otherwise mixed-race Latin Americans: "To borrow a phrase carried over from the last century, 'one drop,' Americans are categorized as Black if they have any African ancestry. On the island of the Dominican Republic, for instance, one can make a sick joke that it's quite the opposite. If you are born with a drop of European blood, you're white" (locations 2470–73). Maternal and paternal DNA results for Cepeda and several of her relatives verified the presence of English or Irish, Amazigh (Berber), and North, West, and Central African backgrounds, among others.

Pushback against the hegemonic tinge of the debate concerning Longoria's African DNA was also evident and eventually led to antiessentialist pronouncements concerning race that stood to counterhegemonically destabilize notions of racial purity and potentially, as Watts cautions, to hegemonically obscure the material effects of racial classifications, including the racist/colorist dimension evident in this group's negotiations of Latinidad. One discussant wrote, "Wow how racist, you cannot even let the woman be 3 percent black African. It's only 3 percent. Blacks were all over Mexico. And who cares if intermarriage was banned. [B]lacks could inter marry the [I]ndians and the mixed Indians could cohabitate with whites." According to another commentator, Eva Longoria's racial mixture can be described as "TYPICAL Mexican aka MESTIZA." In the antiessentialist category, a participant asserted, "Race is a social construct. What does exist is genetics based on geographical-ancestry." Concurred another, "Race is a myth. . . . WTF does European, Asian, and African DNA look like? No such thing, there is no scientific basis for race."

The desire for Native American ancestry runs through the PBS celebrity profile series. On *African American Lives*, Gates notes that testing showed less such ancestry than guests anticipated. Indeed, sociologist Sarah Lawrence-Lightfoot, who claimed African and Native American ancestry, found to her surprise that her ethnic ancestry test revealed no trace of indigenous genetics. The experience of an *African American Lives* viewer on Television without Pity bears out this pattern: "I took one of those DNA tests and wasn't at all surprised to find that my origins are African and Indo-European. I was shocked to find out that I didn't have a drop of Native American blood since one of my family stories is that my great-grandmother was a full-blooded Sioux Indian. That news upsets my mother to this day and she swears that the test is wrong, not the family history." However, in both *African American Lives* and *African American Lives 2*, Gates stresses that some Native Americans owned slaves and occasionally returned slaves who escaped from their captors. In "Genomics en Route," Katharina Schramm discusses an analogous situation that can arise when African Americans seek genetic matches with African peoples. Because of their perceived history as warriors who fought against European hegemony, African Americans can have strong identifications with the Zulu people of South Africa, claiming a cultural affinity that may or may not be supported by genetic ancestry. When Oprah Winfrey's DNA test on *African American Lives* revealed her descent from the Kpelle people of modern-day Liberia, she retained her cultural affinity with the Zulus but also pledged allegiance to her closer genetic cousins.

On the 2012 *Finding Your Roots* episode featuring Branford Marsalis and Harry Connick Jr., the issue of African Americans overestimating their Native American origins again arises. Gates asks several men in a barbershop to predict their percentages of black, white, and native ancestry, noting that many African Americans speak of having relatives with high cheekbones and straight black hair. Chris Everett also observes this tendency, declaring it a "contrived defense mechanism employed by . . . individuals of partial African heritage to hide or disguise racial identity in an oppressive social climate" (369). A Television without Pity poster echoed this perspective on a thread devoted to *African American Lives*: "Among whites, 'Indian' was code for 'black.' Only, some people understood the code while others, particularly in the last couple of generations, didn't. So a lot of people really think they have Cherokee great-great grandmothers."

African Americans wishing to obscure European heritage appear to have adopted a similar strategy. For the men in the barbershop, autosomal tests by 23andMe reveal less indigenous and more European ancestry than predicted. After learning that he is more than 50 percent European, one man says, "It's all about how you look. . . . Next time I get pulled over for driving while black, I'm gonna tell the officer I'm white, man." Marsalis also learns his admixture, but Connick, who is white, is not tested, pinpointing African Americans as another target market for autosomal testing.

The Generations Project mostly indirectly references genetic ancestry. One exception occurs in a 2012 episode featuring Ed, a middle-aged adoptee who looks Native American and has always identified as such. A member of his adoptive family proclaims the importance of this identification to Ed despite the family's apparently evangelical LDS faith. Ed had previously obtained DNA results that showed no Native American ancestry, but after retesting by a different firm, he gathers his adoptive family to report new results: he is one quarter Native American. The episode thus also markets ethnic ancestry testing to another group of consumers—adoptees.

While the genetic ancestry results of Gates's celebrity guests certainly indicate variability in racial categories, these texts do not plainly articulate the distinctions between ethnic ancestry and race as deftly as the PBS website for *African American Lives* (see "Race and Science"). With the exception of those individuals specifically linked to African tribes, continental autosomal classifications dominate all of the studied TV series prior to 2013. The last episode of the 2014 season of *Finding Your Roots* takes stock of the program's use of DNA testing, touts genetic ancestry's new ability to tie subjects to more specific locations, but fails to supply the needed caveats. During the 2016 season, for instance, Mexican American author Sandra Cisneros receives a breakdown of her indigenous background that includes genetic affinity with the Mayans. On *Family Tree* (2013), Tom Chadwick receives more specific results tying his ancestry to particular countries (based on genetic ancestry props provided by an actual testing service in Britain; see "International Biosciences"). Although companies providing genetic ancestry testing have now made their categories more specific, corroboration of most of the narrower designations with continental and consequently racial categories is a likely outcome.

As Squires argues, hybridity's potential to undermine purity narratives is not always realized. These television representations indicate that revelations of genetic hybridity can shake up one's sense of identity in both hegemonic and counterhegemonic ways. However, people in these shows clearly regard autosomal and occasionally haplogroup classifications as analogous to racial ones, implying that all are biological certainties. Conversely, these individuals do not simply jettison strong cultural affinities when DNA testing shows different results.

Genealogy television tends to depict kinship as fundamentally genetic. The title *Who do You Think You Are?* implies that one's genealogy *is* who he/she is. DNA testing providers also play off this fundamentalist view, as evidenced in TV ads for AncestryDNA. One proclaims that the test will "answer, once and for all, what it is that makes you, you," and another depicts a man who trades in his lederhosen for a kilt when a DNA test reveals that he is Scottish rather than German.

Consistent with the message of such ads, *Finding Your Roots* (2016) punctuates a running undercurrent of the genre—that identifying one's genetic ancestors is critical to understanding one's identity. In this instance, DNA testing and matching first indicate that the maternal grandparents who helped bring up actor/rapper/TV host LL Cool J were not his progenitors and subsequently lead to the identification of the individuals who were. The grandparents he knew had adopted his mother and never told her. The names on his family tree suddenly alter before our eyes, even though he thoughtfully admits that the grandparents who raised him were his grandparents "in spirit." However, when he learns that some men in his biological family line were involved with boxing, he mentions his interest in the sport and use of boxing imagery on one of his album covers. He then wonders to Gates whether DNA carries "shadows or consciousness." Seeming to affirm this notion, Gates nods and responds, "Coded."

Relative Race (BYUtv, 2016–) and *Long Lost Family* (TLC, 2016–) have genetic frameworks for kinship as their bedrock, with other family constructs coming in second. In both series, the primary purpose of DNA testing is not determining ethnic ancestry but rather identifying guests' living kin. The need to make a biological link is palpable, and participants do not separate biological from cultural inheritance. The programs seldom fail to highlight common interests or talents of the united or reunited genetic kin, as in an episode of *Long Lost Family* in which a woman and her newfound father share a commitment to animal welfare. On this series, adoption or occasionally hidden paternity has typically played a role in separating genetically related family members, whom the show brings together as adults. Adoptive family members rarely appear, and when they do, their concerns about their adopted relative making the connection are apparently resolved off-screen, most likely as a *precondition* for the adoptee's participation. In one case, an adoptive father expresses reservations about his son meeting his birth mother, but the next thing we observe is the happy union of the genetic mother and son. On *Relative Race*, DNA testing makes some connections across the lines of adoption of one of the family members being united or another that occurred earlier in the line of descent, establishing the family contours if not a specific identification of the biological parent(s). In the second season, the show promoted genetic relatedness in the vein of *Long Lost Family*, with two contestants introduced to very close yet previously unmet relations—one with a sister, the other with both a sister and a father. To punctuate this emphasis, a swirling double helix graphic accompanied by the chorus of "We Are Family," originally recorded by the (biological) sisters of Sister Sledge, frequently transition the program in and out of commercial breaks. In the first season, the winning interracial couple announces that they will use their prize money to begin IVF treatments to produce genetic offspring.

Although neither program overtly assails adoption, revelations on *Long Lost Family* (2016) dramatically emphasize occasions when biological parents did not freely choose to give their children up for adoption. Whether or not DNA tests figure into the family unions featured in an episode, there is no mistaking that the making of genetic connections is the primary goal in every instance. Episode titles such as "Am I Who I Think I Am?" imply genetic identity's authenticity. Other titles, such as "Everything Your Parents Told You Was a Lie," "I've Been Waiting for This Call for Forty-Five Years," and "Your Mom's Been Here the Whole Time" appear to implicate adoptive and other parents who hide or misrepresent a child's genetic origins or suggest that the genetic parent has been waiting with open arms. In "Everything Your Parents Told You Was a Lie," a woman seeks her biological mother, who, it turns out, gave her baby up for adoption because the conception was the result of kidnapping and rape. On closer inspection, this narrative not only privileges nurture over nature and vindicates the biological mother for making this choice but also justifies the behavior of the adoptive parents, who seemed to have gone the extra mile to keep their daughter from uncovering the circumstances of her birth. However, an overall reading of this program that questions the legitimate kinship of adoptive families is not difficult to imagine. A viewer on the *TV Guide* forum for the UK version of the program offered a corresponding critique: "Good program, but not at all realistic. We all like happy endings, but that is not real life. How about showing episodes where the birth mother doesn't want to get involved. Oh I forgot that doesn't make good viewing does it. I am a[n] adoptee who traced my birth mother purely out of curiosity. She was OK, but not all the hearts and roses that the program portrays. Get real."

Television series are not the only traditional media containing pivotal representations of genetic ancestry. Some traditional media, if not most of their negotiations on social media, precede the completion of the Human Genome Project and the widespread appearance of genetic ancestry testing services. Nevertheless, they endeavor to educate and intrigue the audience with this science, thereby setting the stage for the successful marketing of such services.

In 2002, American geneticist Spencer Wells published *The Journey of Man: A Genetic Odyssey*, inspiring a *National Geographic* documentary of the same title that first aired on PBS in 2003. Wells holds a doctorate in biology from Harvard University and engaged in postdoctoral research at Stanford with esteemed Italian geneticist Luigi Luca Cavalli-Sforza and others. Since 2005, Wells has served as director of the National Geographic Society's Geno-graphic Project, a genetic anthropological effort to collect DNA from persons throughout the world to map the migratory patterns of Homo sapiens since their departure from Africa approximately seventy thousand years ago.

In the documentary, Wells travels to various locations, tracing the key pat-terns of human migration around the world; exploring its mysteries; meeting with geneticists, anthropologists, and other scientists; and interacting with members of local populations, some of whom provided DNA samples for his research. The documentary punctuates the book's deliberate use of the word *Man* in the title. Twice Wells proclaims, "The journey of man is the journey of everyone." However, he also pauses halfway through the narra-tive to illuminate the word's significance in the DNA testing used to map human migration patterns. Such testing primarily examines Y-DNA, which, as Wells explains, does not undergo the reshuffling of paternal and maternal genetic contributions as it passes from generation to generation but remains virtually unchanged except for the occasional mutation (marker) that oper-ates as a signpost of approximate place and relative time in efforts to trace human migration. According to Wells, Y-DNA is thus distinct and amenable to his goals, but he ignores the fact that mtDNA, which only females pass on, similarly does not reshuffle and consequently does not explain why mtDNA is not also applicable to his research. The unstated reason, however, is that mtDNA is even more stable and representative of deep ancestry than Y-DNA, as its informative markers are fewer and farther between and consequently reflect a smaller degree of differentiation among populations.

In a later segment, Wells travels to war-torn Kazakhstan to visit a test subject whose Y-DNA exhibits the Central Asian Marker that is considered the "missing link" of human migration science, since it is very old and found in almost every major population beyond Africa. As the man blushes and his family looks on approvingly (women and children peek in from the doorway), and photos of his father and patrilineal grandfather are displayed, a scarcely seen female translator (one of the few women who speak in the film) assists in flattering him and his masculinity. Wells refers to the "history he holds in his blood"—that is, a Y-DNA mutation that traces back forty thousand years to a "very important man."

Catherine Nash's essay, "Genetic Kinship," critiques University of Oxford genetics professor Bryan Sykes's book, *The Seven Daughters of Eve* (2001), as well as a British radio series featuring Sykes, *Surnames, Genes, and Genealogy* (BBC, 2001). In the series, Sykes and several other men with the same surname seek to determine if they share a common ancestor along the direct paternal line. Nash unpacks the gendered implications of the Y-DNA and surname studies reflected in the program: "Though geneticists acknowledge that the Y-chromosome only makes up about 2 percent of an individual man's genotype, by emphasizing its significance as a marker of genetic similarity and diversity, the Y-chromosome seems to stand for *all* that is inherited" (11). Of the production, which is very similar in orientation to *The Journey of Man*, Nash maintains, "Women are absent not just as subjects of research, as a potentially interested audience, and as contributors to the discussion, but also as participants in the process of human reproduction" (9).

Amazon reviewers offer similar comments regarding *The Journey of Man* DVD. One respondent resistively discerned the near symbolic annihilation (see Tuchman) of women in the documentary, noting, "Women were giving birth all the way." Another observed that the documentary should have provided the explanation concerning Y-DNA earlier so that she did not feel so "excluded."

Issues of race gradually bubble to the surface in the documentary, at first unintentionally and then more directly. Wells seeks to determine how some early migrants who left Africa managed to venture all the way to Australia, where they eventually became the Aborigines, without leaving archaeological evidence. He posits that they undertook a coastal migration that would have wiped away such evidence, including along the shoreline of the Indian subcontinent. The Aborigines he meets disagree, however, citing their origin stories, which hold not only that the Aborigines originated in Australia but that all humanity arose from them. When Wells explains that Aborigines and all humans originated in Africa, an Aboriginal man pointedly asks why it could not have happened the other way around. Wells offers a plainly inaccurate as well as inferentially racist response: because they do not have origin stories, "Europeans" use science to answer such questions—the "European way of looking at the world." One Amazon reviewer correctly countered Wells's claim, stating that the creation of origin stories is a "universal act among humans." Nonetheless, Wells confirms his theory of coastal migration by locating the characteristic Aboriginal marker in the Y-DNA of a southern Indian man. But an Indian geneticist helps Wells do so, thereby implicitly disproving his insinuation that science is somehow the special province of Europeans.

Anthropologist Nina Jablonski, one of only two authoritative female images and voices in *The Journey of Man*, subsequently elucidates what we understand as the racial differentiation that took place as the result of migrations into Europe. Differentiations resulting from other migrations, however, remain unexplained. The African ancestors of all humans had skin that was dark with melanin, Jablonski reminds us. Once in Europe, where sunlight is scarcer, darker skin and the need to wear more clothing in the colder climates diminished sun exposure and absorption, which, in turn, compromised the synthesis of vitamin D vital for healthy life and reproduction. Consequently, individuals with somewhat lighter skin were more likely to survive, while those in coastal populations remained a bit darker because they could acquire vitamin D from fish. The explanation, while accurate, links lighter skin with the continental racial designation *European* in a scientific, evolutionary context without clarifying that other factors have determined exactly where we have drawn the lines of demarcation between and among racial categories.

Near the end of the documentary, Wells heads to northeastern Siberia to visit a nomadic tribe said to have generated the small band of travelers who first traversed the Bering land bridge approximately fifteen thousand years ago and spearheaded a migration substantially contributing to the presence of indigenous peoples in the Americas.[1] He later brings news of this connection to Navajo tribe members in the western United States, where the issue of origin stories again arises. According to Navajo belief, the tribe originated on the same land where they have always lived and where they remain today. As one Navajo explains their worldview, Wells utters the word *myth*. A Navajo man challenges Wells, asking, "Why do you call it a myth?" Wells replies, "My bias as a scientist is that I like to see evidence of things." His clumsy interactions with both the Australian Aborigines and the Navajos are reminiscent of the episode of *Family Tree* in which Tom Chadwick believes that a female ancestor was Native American and consequently fetishizes the Mojave tribe members he encounters in a somewhat self-congratulatory fashion. In *The Journey of Man*, Wells ultimately shows the Navajos photos of members of the Siberian tribe from which they purportedly derive, and they seem to concur that a resemblance exists.

As *The Journey of Man* draws to a close, Wells proclaims, "We are all Africans under the skin. . . . Old-fashioned concepts of race are not only divisive but scientifically wrong." However, acknowledgment of or responsibility for the racism that this science enables is absent. As he speaks, the headshots of people of every variety and hue flicker in and out. Nevertheless, some viewers remained dubious and mired in a racist mind-set that rose to overt levels.

One commentator on YouTube wondered: "Did this video just imply that Black Africans are the most prehistoric humans to date? Closest to monkeys? Ironic?" An Amazon user was more "scientific": "The record of science and civilization shows a stark contrast between races. . . . 99.5% of all scientific advances and great works of art and music are from European people. . . . '[P]rejudice' is not the cause, it is the effect." Another Amazon reviewer had "reservations about the certainty with which Dr. Wells approaches his subject, and most particularly the sermonizing at the end about how 'we are all one'. This is Barack Obama territory." The poster suggested that the documentary should have admitted that its science was "theory only." Another user answered this criticism counterhegemonically, declaring, "I find absolutely no contradiction between my Christian faith and the science on which this video is based. And, by the way, I am a Lutheran pastor."

Keith Wailoo specifically points to *The Journey of Man* as contributing to a discourse of genetic ancestry that appears to negate cultural and societal factors as informing one's search for identity (locations 220–30). Similarly, Nash asserts, "Self-declared anti-racist, liberal scientists who repeat the argument that genetic research dispels the myth of pure, discrete 'races', seem unwilling to acknowledge the implications of newly constructed genetic kinship for existing social relations or for understanding the ways genetics is inevitably implicated in ideas of personhood, nationhood, cultural belonging, identity and community" ("Genetic Kinship" 15).

In "Genetic Kinship," Nash also offers a critique of *The Seven Daughters of Eve*, which accounts for prehistoric populations, their migratory movements, and their connection to persons alive today in terms of maternally bestowed, nonrecombining mtDNA. Nash questions whether the attention to mtDNA provided rebuts her criticisms of "masculinism" in *Surnames, Genes, and Genealogy*, which is analogous to *The Journey of Man*.

Seven Daughters chronicles the efforts of geneticists, particularly Sykes, to catalog the genetic "clan mothers," or most recent common maternal ancestors, whose characteristic markers generated each of the haplogroups representing the mtDNA inheritance of most indigenous Europeans. Sykes clarifies that each clan mother must have given birth to at least two daughters, who would then reproduce daughters, and so on, to render her the most recent common maternal ancestor of the clan. In turn, Sykes asserts that these clan mothers descend from the theoretical *Mitochondrial Eve*, or the common maternal ancestor of all humans. However, *Seven Daughters* does not stop there. It goes on to brand each of these clan mothers with a name beginning with the letter of her associated haplogroup and narrativizes her

life in an anthropologically and scientifically informed fiction of birth, sur-
vival, reproduction, and death in the appropriate geographic location and
prehistoric age (between forty-five thousand and ten thousand years ago).

Nash contends that *Seven Daughters* is certainly "full of fertile women"
("Genetic Kinship" 17). Here, she alludes to the claim that the veneration of
women simply for procreating ultimately does little to unsettle hegemonic
gender regimes. In response to the reverence written into Sykes's literary
encounter with "Tara," the mother of his clan, and other ancestors along
this direct maternal lineage, Nash observes, "Pulling the puppet strings of
genetic connection this mother's son becomes master of ceremonies and
master of all the maternal ancestors. The knowing masculine subject wakes
up the passive feminine objects of knowledge" (19).

Nash also interrogates Sykes's punctuating statement, "I feel closer to
these people than to the others," as claiming a genetic affinity with his clan
that supersedes other forms of connection: "Here the supposedly universal
and universally honoured feminine maternal essence is called on to deflect
attention from the dangers of prioritizing biological connection.... Both ma-
ternity and geneticized identities are simultaneously naturalized" ("Genetic
Kinship" 20). Moreover, Nash calls out the elephant in the room: "If 'race'
is cast aside by Sykes and other geneticists like him, biological connection
remains fundamental" (18).

One Amazon reviewer faulted Sykes's book as a platform for further-
ing professional rivalries, particularly in his criticism of Cavalli-Sforza,
and called out its hegemonic ethnocentrism: "If you happen to be from a
non-European race, well, Sykes has got 27 other matrilineal clans sketchily
worked out for you. Still, the Eurocentric, cashocentric Sykes tends to treat
those non-Caucasian ancient mothers as if they were The Twenty-Seven
Stepdaughters of Eve." Indeed, several readers at Goodreads.com incorrectly
gathered from the book that the "seven daughters" were the ancestors of all
humans. An Asian male reader stated that the back cover of his copy claims
that the book addresses the maternal ancestors of all humanity and that he
was disappointed to realize that it features only European clan mothers. In
fact, a blurb on the front cover of at least one printing of the book reads,
"The astonishing story that reveals how *each of us* can trace our genetic
ancestors" (emphasis added).

Somewhat paradoxically, the Amazon poster who referred to the "Twenty-
Seven Stepdaughters of Eve" also appeared to adopt a hegemonic stance that
essentializes race and claims an unbreakable link between it and genetics
that ensures the perpetuation of racism: "Despite all the propaganda that

'race does not exist'—humanity will never get over its obsession with race: Race is Family. A racial group is an extremely extended family that is inbred to some degree."

On Goodreads, a number of *Seven Daughters* readers were clearly scientifically intrigued and informed. Several commented negatively on the fictionalized portion of the book. Wrote one woman, "If you so desire, you may simply ignore the second half of this book as unnecessary filler, an act I wish I had done myself." A male user had the same opinion but acknowledged that the fictional narratives might have been necessary: "The final section is a romanticized emotional presentation of how wonderful it is that we are all at some level related. . . . To my mind this section added little to the import of Sykes work and made it less scientific, a mere gesture to enhance the work's popularity for what Sykes or his publisher felt to be the general reading public." But even this seemingly knowledgeable reader perceived the book as emphasizing that we are *all* related in spite of the fact that it is clearly slanted toward the genetic inheritance of Europeans. Others, such as one female reader, anticipated a more antiessentialist discourse on race: "I do wish there had been much more about the concept of race . . . to dispel this myth of race as skin colour/ethnicity/anything easily identifiable. The implications of that are much more interesting in my opinion than . . . a sense of identity with some woman from 30,000 years ago." However, whereas respondents to the video *Journey of Man* recognized its masculine tilt, whether approvingly or not, most readers of *Seven Daughters* did not point to its gendered disposition, let alone critique it as Nash does in "Genetic Kinship" or in any other explicit terms. Online responses to *Seven Daughters* and *Journey of Man* tip the analysis in the direction of digital media's role in purveying genetic ancestry science, laying the groundwork for its growing role in the practice of family history.

TUBULAR GENEALOGY IV

Identity and Genetic Ancestry in Digital Media and
Related Texts and Practices

DIGITAL MEDIA, GENETIC ANCESTRY, AND IDENTITY

Questions regarding race, ethnicity, and genetic ancestry invite scrutiny
of digitally mediated texts and practices involving genetic ancestry testing
services, their web communication, and associated communities; YouTube
videos and message boards/forums in which genetic ancestry customers
reveal hybridity in their test results; and a selection of those that racialize
and/or advocate racism with the ostensible support of genetic ancestry science. One issue involves whether such digital communication accurately and
completely describes the significance and limits of genetic testing for ethnic
ancestry, especially in relation to cultural inheritance and the prospects
of racist blowback. Another concerns the extent to which such texts, user
responses, and the output of digital media outlets construct or reconstruct
categories by which to designate the ethnic ancestry of participants, reinforce
or challenge essentialist notions of race and/or gender, or warn against the
racist, racializing discourses on the Internet and elsewhere that utilize genetic
ancestry science as evidence.

Alondra Nelson and Won Hwang focus on "roots revelations"—YouTube
videos in which African Americans share various facets of the genetic ancestry testing process typically expected to affirm or otherwise situate their
roots in Africa as well as responses by commentators. Nelson and Hwang
recognize the ubiquitous "reveal" segments of reality TV as well as family
history TV programs as precursors and/or facilitators of the practice and
employ Nelson's earlier concept, *affiliative self-fashioning*, which the authors
describe as the "constitution of individual identity, through and toward the

goal of association with others, including ancestors and DNA 'kin'" (273). Although Nelson and Hwang question the emphasis on genetic as opposed to culturally situated identities, they also acknowledge that these exercises may reflect what John L. Jackson calls *racial sincerity*, or the "race-based yet non-essentialist form of negotiated, interactional identity" (Nelson and Hwang 273).

Taking Nelson and Hwang's lead without inhabiting the same territory, I use two roots-revelatory YouTube videos posted by persons *not* specifically seeking African heritage to assess negotiations of unexpected hybridity in test results as well as overtly and inferentially racist texts and subtexts revealed in the ensuing commentary.

In a fifteen-minute video, "Got my DNA Results from Ancestry.com Part 1," Druana Johnston, who is olive-skinned with dark hair and eyes and appears to be in her thirties, is driving with her children in balmy Baja, California, the climate of which, she explains, is the reason her "family migrated down here from Europe." She discloses the results of her autosomal test from AncestryDNA, declaring that her prior understanding was that she was "half Mexican and half German." The results demonstrate her to be 24 percent Native American (localized in either North or South America) and 73 percent European, including 37 percent British as well as smaller percentages of Italian, Greek, Slavic, and Spanish/Portuguese affinity.

Like the Latina/o celebrities responding to genetic ancestry results in the PBS celebrity profile series, Johnston is astounded at the amount of European in her background. The specificity of newer Ancestry.com subclassifications and the variations in her European ancestry also surprise her, as do the trace amounts of Pacific Islander and North African. She states that her children look white and that her husband plans to have his genetic ancestry assessed. "I would love to be every race," she exclaims, celebrating her hybridity, but reminds us that some people are less accepting: a member of her father's family did not want some facet of their ancestry to be revealed. She suspects that this reluctance relates to the family's "Slavic" origins, which could mean that they were descended from gypsies. Among the very few uniformly uncontroversial comments generated by this video is one that announces, "I always thought you Greek or Italian."

A more strenuously negotiated five-minute YouTube video, "My Ancestry. com DNA Results!," was posted by Anthony B, a white male who appears to be between twenty-five and thirty-five years of age. He has received ethnic ancestry results from AncestryDNA and questions some of the components in his profile. Anthony B reports that his father is Italian and his mother

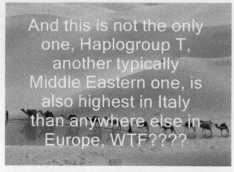

And this is not the only one, Haplogroup T, another typically Middle Eastern one, is also highest in Italy than anywhere else in Europe, WTF????

Figure 6.1: Screen shot ItalianBrownSkin, "Italians White? Since When?" YouTube.com, 18 October 2011.

Polish and that although some of the results coincide with this understanding, others do not. His regional affiliations turn out to be 67 percent Eastern European, 19 percent Southern European, and 12 percent Persian, Turkish, and Caucasus, a finding he calls the "odd ball out," presumably because it crosses over into another racial category. He reasons that this ancestry could derive from his mother's side because of the various "empires" that have been in and out of Poland but also considers that it could be from his father's side because of his father's Persian looks and Italy's proximity to Greece.

Anthony B declares that he looks like his father and finds it hard to believe that he is 67 percent Eastern European. He describes his father's skin color as "olive" and eye color as "hazel," while his mother is blond and fair-skinned with blue eyes. Anthony B announces that he will first have his mother and then possibly his father, take the test to determine where the "odd ball" ancestry is coming from.

Both Anthony and Druana allude to coloring as indicative of race. While neither video creator explicitly discounts cultural inheritance, their matter-of-fact pronouncements confer validity on genetic ancestry tests in a manner that affirms their consequence in identity-seeking endeavors. None of this is inconsistent with Nelson's notion of affiliative self-fashioning. However, Druana, through her embrace of hybridity, seems indifferent to Jackson's conceptualization of racial sincerity as a particular expression of nonessentialist affiliation with marginalized racial identities.

A respondent to Anthony B's video whose thumbnail suggests that she is female and olive-skinned and whose screen name suggests Middle Eastern origins is not surprised but instead celebrates the ethnic hybridity revealed by Anthony B while assuming the ethnic/racial significance of the autosomal classifications reflected in his test results: "Southern European men and women are considered to be the most sexi[e]st Europeans. And you know why they are considered to be the most good looking Europeans? It's because of that Middle Eastern Arab, Turkish, Persian bloodlines they have from ancient times."

In another entry, this same poster argues that Spaniards and Italians have Middle Eastern ancestry, prompting a response from someone all too eager to position Spanish and Italian unequivocally under the umbrella of whiteness and to racialize a label that actually denotes a religion: "[You're] not Italian or Spanish but you envy them. Italians are European as it gets. [M]usic, arts, explorers.... [L]ook what [A]rabs are doing in Europe today. [M]uslim rats." The first poster then defends herself by delving into genetic ancestry, utilizing haplogroup designations to indicate race, equating genetics with culture, and endeavoring to deessentialize whiteness:

> White means NOTHING! ... The North European Americans in the early days of America wanted to divide themselves from other immigrants. So they came up with these ideas of "white," black, brown, etc. ... When those don't exist at all. ... In today's world "white" pretty much means European culture. Anyone that's native to Europe is called "white." So ... Spaniards are white because they are located in Europe. BUT even their European culture has Arabic culture influences. ... What is Western European genetics? LOL! [Y-DNA haplogroups] R_1b, R_1a, J_2 etc. ARE NOT EUROPEAN!!

While this commentator may be somewhat confused about which haplogroups found in Europe are common in the Middle East and what this sort of connection actually means, she is correct that genetic evidence of affinity between many European and Middle Eastern populations exists.

YouTube videos that intentionally employ genetic ancestry evidence in support of racist, racializing claims premised in white privilege and supremacy and their counternarratives are also relevant. One of the areas of Europe that reflects genetic mixture is southern Italy. On YouTube, however, posters have subjected Italians as a whole to racist, racializing discourses. Citing Y-DNA haplogroups, a video posted by "ItalianBrownSkin" under the title "Italians White? Since When?" asserts that the genetics of Italians indicate racial mixing atypical of Northern "legitimate" Europeans and reflect Middle Eastern, including Jewish, ancestry (see figure 6.1).[1] In the video, ominous, vaguely Middle Eastern music accompanies a succession of still color images, including a repeated image of camels caravanning across the desert with varying titles. Other images show highlighted clippings from scientific studies or articles from recognizable news media outlets such as the *New York Times.*

The video not only reflects orientalist assumptions and strategies and serves a racializing function, presumably in keeping with the poster's racist motivations, but reproduces the notion that Y-DNA haplogroups—masculine inheritances that speak to only one lineage—inform the overall genetic ancestry of a person or group. My half-Asian nephew inherited his father's (and my father's) Y-DNA but this hardly represents the totality of his genetic ancestry.

Some YouTube videos bypass genetic ancestry and simply display an array of swarthy Italians to advance this argument that also presumes (lily) white preference and supremacy. Other European nationalities—particularly Greek, Spanish, and Portuguese—are implicated by similarly purposed and premised YouTube videos highlighting genetic evidence and/or images of olive- and brown-skinned people. Video refutations of these postings tend to reproduce their racist premises, employing genetic ancestry and/or a selection of images of blond, blue-eyed, Aryan-looking citizens of the country in question in asserting uncompromising whiteness. In diverging from the text while still reproducing hegemonic meanings regarding the key issue, this response is a *negotiated reading* according to Stuart Hall's *encoding/decoding* scheme for audience analysis ("Encoding/Decoding").

Starting in 2011, other racist, racializing misapplications of genetic ancestry science began to emerge in a spate of YouTube videos and responses surrounding reports that King Tutankhamen's Y-DNA had been determined from his mummified remains to reflect R1b1a2, which is the Y-DNA haplotype most frequently seen among Europeans (see Pappas). Apparently based on a fleeting shot from a Discovery Channel documentary on the Egyptian pharaoh's DNA, a genomics company in Sweden, iGENEA, began advertising on its website that its genetic testing service was a way one might discover shared ancestry with the king. However, while some data relating to Tut's DNA had been published, Y-DNA findings were not among them, a fact that provided grist for conspiracy mills on both sides of the debate.

White supremacists jumped at the chance to claim, with supposedly scientific backing, that whites rather than blacks were responsible for the ancient Egyptian civilization. Those taking exception to this argument often refuted it while reproducing some of its questionable assumptions and implications regarding genetic ancestry science. YouTube videos with such titles as "REAL King Tut DNA Test = BLACK 100%" (Sarahize) and "REAL King Tut DNA

TABLE 6.1: MAJOR US GENETIC ANCESTRY TESTING PROVIDERS, THEIR SERVICES, AND CHARGES, 2013				
Provider	Genographic Project	Family Tree DNA	23andMe	Ancestry DNA
Services	Geno 2.0 package: Y-DNA (for males only); mtDNA, admixture; hominid species (Neanderthal/ Denisovan)	Family Finder (matching/admixture); various levels of mtDNA and Y-DNA ordered separately; combo packages	Package: mtDNA, Y-DNA (for males only), admixture; hominid species (Neanderthal); matching; relatively spare family tree posting	Heavily promoted admixture/matching/ family tree service; Y-DNA/mtDNA ordered separately; combo packages
Cost	$159 for package (temporarily reduced)	$99 for Family Finder; Y-DNA ($59–$359); mtDNA ($59–$199); various combo packages	Package: $99	Admixture/matching/ family tree service: $99; ceased offering Y-DNA and mtDNA services in 2015

Test = WHITE 100%" (Commander Thsh) proliferated, with all accepting the premise that the masculine inheritance, Y-DNA, offers a unique way to account for one's genetic origins. This assumption reinforces the ideas that a single lineage can reflect the totality of one's ancestry, that genetic ancestry designations straightforwardly correspond to constructed racial categories, and that culture and genetics are inseparable.

The Internet sites, including discussion forums, of genetic ancestry testing services (the Genographic Project, Family Tree DNA, 23andMe, AncestryDNA, African Ancestry, and AfricanDNA) also come into play. The information provided on the websites for these services, accurate as of 2014, reflects both similarity and divergence around the issues of what the tests actually do, what the results actually mean, and how they are or should be used and regarded. MyHeritage DNA, which launched in 2016, arrived too late to be included in this assessment. Just as genealogy television does not faithfully represent the carefully calibrated explanation of the relationship of genetic ancestry and racial classifications that PBS uses on its website (see "Race and Science"), the communications of genetic ancestry services do not explain the intricate details of what the testing can and cannot reveal (see table 6.1).[2] For all these services, customers order testing kits online and then collect their own samples and return them by mail. With the exception of African Ancestry, which supplies its product, including certificates and other informative materials, by US mail, test subjects receive an email informing them that the test has been completed; they can then access the results online. Customers collect samples either by swabbing their cheeks and placing the swabs into vials or by spitting directly into the vials; the vials are then mailed back for testing.

The Genographic Project, headed by geneticist Spencer Wells, is a National Geographic Society effort to map human migration patterns through worldwide genetic testing. The project is described as a nonprofit endeavor sponsored by the National Geographic Society, IBM, and the Waitt Foundation, even as National Geographic has become an arm of the Fox media empire under the auspices of conservative mogul Rupert Murdoch. According to the society's website, a portion of the cost of the complete testing package goes to the Genographic Legacy Fund, which "supports community-led indigenous conservation and revitalization projects." Women seeking knowledge of their paternal haplogroup must purchase or solicit the purchase of an additional kit for a male paternal relative. The project's matching with markers of ancient hominid species predating Homo sapiens—that is, Neanderthals and Denisovans—is a distinctive feature. Genetic markers of both species have been identified and recognized in the DNA inheritance of many humans, suggesting that Neanderthals and Denisovans interbred with more dominant Homo sapiens, a discovery that also introduces a plausible explanation for how and why these other hominids died out. Most people with at least some European and/or Asian background will have a small amount (approximately 1–4 percent) of Neanderthal ancestry evident in their genomes, while Denisovan genetic inheritance is less certain and less pervasive.

The Genographic Project's website explains autosomal testing for ethnic ancestry:

> You will also receive a visual percentage breakdown of your genomic ancestry by regional genetic affiliation. These affiliations are compiled by examining the genetic markers across your entire genome beyond mtDNA and the Y chromosome—and comparing your results with our growing database to reveal the regional affiliations of your ancestry. Your regional genetic affiliations reflect the ancient migratory paths of your ancestors and how they mixed with groups around the world.

This explanation meticulously avoids terms such as *race* and *ethnicity* and instead speaks of "affiliation" with various migratory groups. In so doing, however, it also fails to recognize and address potential misinterpretations and abuses of this science.

Customers cannot easily access the breakdown of migratory groups used to present ethnic ancestry until they receive their results. The site warns, "Remember, this is a mixture of both recent (past six generations) and ancient patterns established over thousands of years, so you may see surprising regional percentages." There are nine migratory groups: Northeast Asian, Mediterranean, Southern African, Southwest Asian, Native American, Oceanian, Southeast Asian, Northern European, and Sub-Saharan African. While many of these classifications use continental designations, the site's discussion strives *not* to equate them with specific ethnicities or races but rather to indicate where these populations are most frequently found. For instance, the description for the Southwest Asian migratory group reads, "This component is found at highest frequencies in India and neighboring populations, including Tajikistan and Iran in our reference dataset. It is also found at lower frequencies in Europe and North Africa." Similarly, members of the Mediterranean group, are said to be found in Italy, Greece, Egypt, and Tunisia and to lesser degrees in North Africa, the Middle East, Central and South Asia, and the rest of Europe. By their descriptions if not their titles, such designations do not appear to situate subjects according to continental classifications that are analogous to racial ones. Even with knowledge of relatively recent ancestral origins, a subject who is found to have a large chunk of Mediterranean ancestry, for instance, would not know for sure how much of it associates him/her with the continents of Europe, Asia, or Africa. Consequently, some of this provider's presentations and classifications confound culturally constructed racial categories, perhaps revealing them for what they are. Others may do the same or demonstrate their own constructions by establishing and using ethnic ancestry designations.

The advertising for the Family Finder autosomal and matching service on Family Tree DNA's website freely employs the term *ethnic makeup* as a selling point to consumers and neglects to make additional, appropriate clarifications: "Our Family Finder also has a component called myOrigins. This component gives you a breakdown of your ethnic makeup by percent." A bulleted list of features utilizes continental designations associated with race in proclaiming that the test "provides percentages of your ancestral make-up (Native-American, Middle Eastern (including Jewish), African, West and East European)." It lists the subgroups and populations included under each designation, such as Southern European under European, subsuming Italian, Sardinian, and Tuscan populations. Other bullet points tout the gender-neutral status of the autosomal test as an attractive feature.

Family Tree DNA is a division of the genetic testing company Gene by Gene. Its cofounder, Bennett Greenspan, developed the idea after confronting a brick wall in researching his own family history. Patrons can transfer their data from the Genographic Project's website to Family Tree, which performs the tests for the project. Users might assume that they would then be permitted to utilize Family Tree's matching service at no additional cost, since the Genographic Project does not provide this service. However, when I did this for both my father's and my data, the only result was a restatement of my mtDNA haplogroup. I could not reaffirm my father's mtDNA and Y-DNA haplogroups/haplotypes because only the least expensive of the firm's Y-DNA analyses, which examines a limited number of markers, was included with the transfer. Instead, our personal test data pages featured a comparatively spare explanation of these results and a link with which to purchase Family Tree's autosomal and matching service. Once a test is ordered, patrons have the opportunity to purchase a la carte various analyses of particular, mostly innocuous medical/health-related information, such as a genetic determination concerning the moisture content of one's earwax.

23andMe is a private company cofounded and headed by Anne Wojcicki, who was formerly married to Google cofounder Sergey Brin. Brin and Google have made considerable investments in the enterprise. 23andMe's website publicizes the company's association with *Finding Your Roots* and provides basic explanations regarding an inclusive package that provides mtDNA, Y-DNA (if the test subject is male), autosomal, Neanderthal DNA, matching, and some family tree information. 23andMe offered extensive health-related results prior to late November 2013, when it suspended those tests pending the outcome of two lawsuits alleging that this component required approval from the US Food and Drug Administration (FDA). In addition, the lawsuits argued that the firm was essentially asking customers to pay for the privilege of helping it establish and mine for profit a medical database that benefits researchers looking for correlations between genetic mutations and medical conditions (see Convey; Perrone). The genetic ancestry portion of 23andMe's service continued, and on 21 October 2015, the company announced that a revised version of health-based testing would resume with FDA approval (see Pollack).

AncestryDNA and other providers also can sell their aggregated data (see Cooke), and critics worry that employers, insurance companies, and others might misappropriate such data by asking potential customers or employees to detail their genetic predisposition to disease found through genomic testing. This prospect has a racial/ethnic dimension in that certain diseases are associated with particular groups, such as Tay-Sachs (Ashkenazi Jews) and sickle cell anemia (Africans, Indians, and Arabs). Iceland's digital *Íslendingabók* and associated genetic database had been canaries in the coal mine for controversies surrounding the collection of genealogical and genetic ancestry related data in health-related contexts, and some Icelanders obtained the right to opt out for privacy or other reasons (see Shanks; Creet).

23andMe's marketing privileges the European category as an example of how individual regions are broken down: "Find out what percent of your DNA comes from populations around the world, ranging from East Asia, Sub-Saharan Africa, Europe, and more. Break European ancestry down into distinct regions such as the British Isles, Scandinavia, Italy and Ashkenazi Jewish. People with mixed ancestry, African Americans, Latina/os, and Native Americans will also get a detailed breakdown." The complete breakdown scheme is not easily accessible until results are in, at which time subjects can view the test's twenty-three categories, almost all of which are continental indicators with associated regional populations. However, the specificity of population breakdowns differs among the categories, and the apparent promise of such breakdowns for Latina/os and Native Americans is misleading. Native American is just one category under the East Asian and Native American classification, and the Latina/o designator does not appear on the list. Instead, patrons can determine such mixed ancestry by the combination of continental categories and subcategories represented in a subject's results.

AncestryDNA, the genetic ancestry service associated with Ancestry.com, now heavily promotes an admixture and matching service and has ceased offering mtDNA and Y-DNA tests. Because Ancestry.com already posts numerous family trees, customers can often examine the trees of their genetic matches for shared geographic locations and family names and potentially establish or confirm a family connection that fills in missing tree branches. The service's admixture categories, which were recalibrated in 2013, thereby altering the ethnic ancestry designations and percentages of existing patrons, are now continental (with the exception of Pacific Islander) and include numerous subpopulations, many of which are the names of countries. For instance, the Africa designation corresponds with subgroups in Nigeria, Senegal, Cameroon/Congo, and Ivory Coast/Ghana, among others. A video on the site proclaims that the testing provides "estimates for your genetic ethnicity by comparing your DNA to the DNA of other people who are native to a region," implying a connection between ethnicity and geographic populations while hedging those bets by using the term *estimates*.

African Ancestry differs from the other services by specializing in the identification of African regional and sometimes tribal ancestry through matching. It focuses on maternal- and paternal-line testing as the basis for such matching and boasts possession of the largest database used for such purposes. In an effort to disassociate admixture classifications from racial ones, the website explains, "Your ancestral mix report includes the percentages of African, European, Indigenous American, East Asian, and Indian ancestry that you have. YOU WILL NOT LEARN COUNTRIES OR ETHNIC GROUPS." Of course, the continental designations enable patrons to assume racial categories. The site also permits people who already had their mtDNA and/or Y-DNA tested but came away with no regional or tribal matches to transfer their data for matching—for a fee, of course. Two African Americans of Nigerian origin, Gina Page and Dr. Rick Kittles, founded African Ancestry in 2003.

Another firm that specializes in African-ancestry DNA testing, AfricanDNA, plays up its autosomal test and an endorsement by Henry Louis Gates Jr. While the website is somewhat cagey about the firm's associations, AfricanDNA is an affiliate of Family Tree DNA and utilizes its testing and matching apparatuses.

Discussion groups on 23andMe and Ancestry.com are available to all logged-in patrons. On 23andMe, many are devoted to topics related to the health information provided by the service; on Ancestry.com, many address the conventional family-tree building aspect of the site. Threads that reference DNA testing for ethnic ancestry or paternal/maternal-line testing highlight particular haplogroups, discuss ethnicity outcomes, ask technical questions, and feature complaints about the service in question or its competitors. Some technical questions involve associating DNA results with Family Tree Maker software, GEDCOM files, or GEDMatch.com. (GedMatch is a free site for uploading DNA data from Family Tree DNA or 23andMe [but not AncestryDNA] for additional analysis and matching.)

Many threads on both sites reflect customers' frustration concerning genetic matches that have no trees or private trees or do not follow up on invitations to share. When it comes to particular ethnicities revealed by autosomal testing, Native American and Middle Eastern seem to create the most dialogue, with participants disappointed that their understanding of their own Native American ancestry is not borne out in the autosomal tests and others reacting with everything from curiosity to concern about Middle Eastern background revealing itself through such tests. These reactions are consistent with similar ones on family history television and in YouTube videos and are often explained in similar ways, such as the association of Sicilians and other southern Italians with Middle Eastern migratory paths.

One 23andMe thread reflected a riveting, unfolding narrative. The patron who began it had a very close DNA match with someone he did not know. After he revealed the contours of the data in question, other participants informed him that this could only be a paternal relationship. His father—at least, the father he knew—was deceased. Some suggested that the match was not necessarily the result of anything illicit but could mean that his father had an identical twin who was given up for adoption or that the original poster was conceived using a sperm donor. When the man explained that he had taken the test to obtain medical information, others encouraged him to resolve the issue for this reason but argued that doing so did not need to change his existing understanding of his family. When the man initiated a dialogue with the match, he admitted to having donated sperm. The patron then initiated a discussion with his mother, who disclosed that she and his father had indeed used a sperm donor after failing to conceive.

The man concluded that this information did not alter his family affinities but wondered why his father had spoken as if his son was a genetic relative, noting personality characteristics he shared with his paternal grandfather. These characteristics, however, could easily have been cultural inheritances. Moreover, the episode bears out Lee Rainie and Barry Wellman's assertion that "expertise is more in dispute" for today's networked individual, creating more "uncertainty about whom and what information sources to trust" and the propensity to "turn to . . . social networks to make sense" of voluminous and often conflicting data (locations 577–86).

GENETIC ANCESTRY: THE JOURNEY OF ME

Because of its scientific raison d'être, the Genographic Project seemed like the best route for exploring my genetic ancestry, and had I not been doing research, I probably would have stopped there. I took the test, which uses the cheek-swabbing method. To determine my Y-DNA haplogroup and assess differences in our autosomal results, I then purchased a second testing kit for my father. My results did not materialize for two full months, while my father's took a bit longer. Along the way, I received email notifications of the tests' progress.

When my results were available on the website, I discovered that my mtDNA haplogroup is U3a. Site information and further exploration told me that the U3 classification is rare in Europe, with the highest levels found near the Black Sea and eastern Mediterranean. U3a arose more than twenty-one thousand years ago. However, Bryan Sykes does not feature U3 in *The Seven Daughters of Eve*'s catalog of the "clan mothers" of today's Europeans. Rather, U5 (which Sykes nicknames Ursula) is the only U subgroup included in the book. Apparently, Sykes eventually got around to giving U3 a nickname: Uma. On the website, haplogroup results are accompanied by a series of maps containing the migratory routes that terminate with one's specific haplogroup. After an Internet search to learn more about U3 and its subgroups, however, I realized that more information was available regarding U5 and other predominantly European mtDNA groupings.

According to the Genographic Project, my autosomal "ethnic ancestry" results are 60 percent Mediterranean; 20 percent Southwest Asian; and 18 percent Northern European. My Neanderthal ancestry is approximately 2 percent. According to the information provided when reviewing results on the website, Southwest Asian is most associated with India and nearby populations, including Iran. The Mediterranean category primarily covers Italy, Greece, Egypt, and Tunisia. The eclecticism of these categories prevents users from readily equating racial identity with genetic designations and confers a deessentializing ambiguity in terms of both constructed racial classifications and the demarcations favored by the testing service. However, the service also fails to acknowledge or address the likelihood that patrons will make associations between race and genetic populations.

My father's autosomal mixture approximates mine, although there are slightly higher Mediterranean, Southwest Asian, and Neanderthal percentages as well as a slightly lower Northern European one. Unlike me, he shows trace amounts of Denisovan. The Genographic Project apparently had no maps or other information or graphics that extended to my father's specific Y-DNA haplotype, presumably because it is a newly established offshoot of the very ancient G haplogroup with a long, alphanumeric designation. Nothing appeared on the Internet about this specific subcategory, but G2a3, defined by the L30 mutation, is its direct root. L30 appears to have started in the Mediterranean region (as defined by the Genographic Project) and is today concentrated in areas around the Black Sea. My father's mtDNA links him to haplogroup H7, a relatively rare subclade of haplogroup H that arose in West Asia and can be found most frequently in Romania and elsewhere around the Black Sea as well as in Italy, Portugal, England, Ireland, and portions of the Middle East and North Africa.

Next on the agenda was AncestryDNA. Since I already had a family tree posted on Ancestry.com (though it had not been recently updated), Ancestry's admixture test and matching service had the potential to help me fill in missing information by examining the locations and surnames connected to the trees of my genetic matches. However, I found that my tree was more

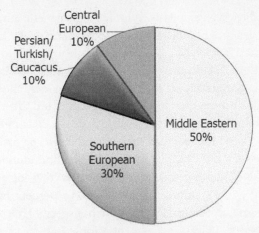

Figure 6.2: My first DNA results from AncestryDNA.

complete than those of matches whose trees were not designated as private, so, I stood to help them more than they stood to help me.

The first ethnic ancestry results I received from Ancestry informed me that I am 50 percent Middle Eastern, 30 percent Southern European, 10 percent Central European, and 10 percent Persian, Turkish, and Caucasus (see figure 6.2). The percentage of Middle Eastern ancestry was surprising, given the seemingly divergent results provided by the Genographic Project. Insofar as I was writing about hybridity and the constructedness of racial classifications, however, the inconsistency between the two results proved a point. Results from the various testing services can disagree because each examines a somewhat different set of ancestry informative markers (AIMS), different numbers of AIMS, and/or AIMS representing varying numbers of past generations. The tests also disagree because of varying classification schemes and the number of relevant samples collected.

In 2013, however, AncestryDNA recalibrated its categories and results. I received an email that alerted me that my reconfigured ethnic ancestry categories and percentages were 70 percent European (64 percent Italy/ Greece, 2 percent Iberian Peninsula, 2 percent Ireland. 1 percent England, and >1 percent European Jewish) and 30 percent West Asian (25 percent Near East, 5 percent Caucasus). According to an accompanying map, the Near East category subsumes Saudi Arabia, Iraq, Iran, Turkey, Syria, and parts of Egypt, inclusions that help to reconcile the new results with the old. "Italy/Greece" had also apparently encompassed some of the Middle Eastern category, possibly via an emphasis on more recent genetic mutations and the logic that the genetics of Italians and Greeks automatically include Middle Eastern affinities. However, because most people understand "Italy/Greece" to be part of Europe, customers who so identify need not confront a large slice of Middle Eastern pie on their pie chart. Providers thus can reshuffle categories to favor more specific and recent origins and thereby minimalize racially underpinned reactions from some majority consumers.

23andMe's test, which, like Ancestry's, uses the spitting method of collection, confirmed my mtDNA haplotype to be U3a and found a comparable percentage of Neanderthal ancestry. After a slight revision to reflect more detailed study, 23andMe declared that I am 83.7 percent European (73.6 percent Southern European and 10.1 percent nonspecific), 3.4 percent Middle Eastern and North African (2.2 percent Middle Eastern, .5 percent North African, .6 percent nonspecific), and 13 percent unassigned. A more specific breakdown of European ancestry revealed 53.5 percent Italian, 20 percent nonspecific Southern European, and 10.1 percent nonspecific European. These results seemed to align with the modified results from AncestryDNA. It is not clear whether the results indicating Italian and Southern European affinities automatically subsume likely Middle Eastern associations, and the trace amounts of Sub-Saharan African initially detected by the test had vanished.

Knowledge of my test results has generated some noteworthy interactions with family members, other test subjects, and those who happen to be both. Both old and new social media—specifically, the telephone, US mail and, most conveniently, Facebook—provided mechanisms to put me and two of my siblings in touch with what Rainie and Wellman characterize as "far-flung" relations (location 441). In this case, we had not had contact with these cousins for decades, but family history, the declining health of our remaining parents, and social media motivated and facilitated such rapprochement. Consequently, genetic ancestry presented yet another opportunity to share. Since my mother's brother and sister married a sister and brother who were my father's first cousins, several newly reconnected cousins are genetically related to me on both sides of my family. We share three sets of great-grandparents, making them both my first and second cousins.

When I received my results from the Genographic Project, I informed some members of my close family about the results in person and by email, and they responded with interest, intrigue, and a series of pertinent and appropriately skeptical questions. Next, I clicked on the Genographic Project's link that allowed me to instantly share the results on Facebook. In response to these revelations, one of these first/second cousins related that a Turkish man had encountered him on the street, certain that the two of them shared Turkish origins. Another cousin made a skeptical reference to human evolution, and others had perfunctory responses or none at all.

In the arena of genetics versus culture, such interactions are as apt or even more apt to underscore cultural dissimilarities as they are to accentuate genetic affinities. For instance, some family members may be unable to entertain the reality of mtDNA mutations that occurred ten thousand years ago because they believe that human beings, the earth, and the entire universe did not exist at that time. Religious as well as political divergences, then, stand to unhinge connections otherwise based on genetics alone. However, in this case, such reconnection ultimately drove home the realization that the love of and/or professional or avocational expertise in music that has seemingly been passed down from generation to generation along this family lineage is most assuredly a *cultural* inheritance. The role of genetics in such affinities and aptitudes, if there is one, is currently indeterminable. Further, genetic inheritance is negligible once one moves beyond third or fourth great-grandparents, meaning that cultural inheritance has a greater potential for lasting influence.

Moreover, not all family-related advances in biomedical science emphasize genetic affinity. For example, as Peter Wade argues, assisted reproductive technologies can bypass genetic relationships entirely—for example, when an embryo biologically produced by one couple is implanted into the uterus of another female. Such science recognizes a blurring of distinctions among genetics, biology, and culture.

Most Latina/os and African Americans on family history television have not welcomed genetic evidence of European ancestry but rather have circumscribed it based on cultural realizations of unequal power relations. While the cultural inheritance of musical knowledge and interest is not the same as understanding one's place in cultural regimes of power, genealogy and genetic ancestry do offer the potential to accomplish the latter.

The family (and other) connections made thus far through the matching services of both AncestryDNA and 23andMe have ranged from logical to curious to intriguing, whether academically speaking or otherwise. In each case, the service lists matches by estimated closeness. Contacting another patron requires asking the testing service to send an invitation; if the second patron accepts, the two individuals can then exchange information via the site and ultimately by other means if they so choose. If a patron's family tree is designated as private, only authorized patrons can access it.

In my case, one service matched me to another patron who was my first/
second cousin (my mother's sister's child). Buttressing perceptions of scientific validity, this cousin shared my mtDNA haplogroup first determined
through the Genographic Project. I received another invitation from a patron whom the service predicted to be a second cousin and who shared my
mother's very unusual maiden name. After I accepted his invitation, I was
able to access his family tree and confirm that he was indeed my second
cousin. Having gained access on the site to his Y-DNA haplotype, I could
then associate it with my maternal grandfather and other relations along
this direct paternal line and by extrapolation with my mother. This second
cousin and I exchanged email addresses and chatted beyond the site about
our particular branches of the larger family tree. He then transmitted my
email address to his elderly uncle, my mother's first cousin, who contacted
me to ask about my mother and her siblings.

Far-flung relations who helped in supplying missing genealogical information also emerged. The service connected me with another patron
predicted to be a distant cousin with a shared a location in Italy and surname.
Although our trees did not extend back far enough to identify a shared ancestor, we were reasonably certain that one existed. Another patron matched as
a distant cousin offered the name of a town in Italy that I determined to be
within thirty-five kilometers of the ancestral town in the region of Campania
of my maternal line great-grandparents. As this patron's information was
sketchy and my information concerning this lineage was similarly sketchy
(the ancestral town was the one that refused to allow the LDS church to film
its records), no further linkage was possible. Finally, I was connected with a
man predicted to be a distant cousin who was searching for the identity of
his birth father. He related to me the time frame and general location for his
conception. However, our closest possible relationship was fifth cousin, and
my family tree currently contains no cousins beyond level 3. I explained to
him that although I had many relations who were in that vicinity at about
that time, our common ancestor, if there was one, lived generations ago. I
suggested that a surname from my tree might match his father's and that he
was welcome to look, but I never heard anything else from him. His query
reinforces the idea that people may take these tests for a variety of reasons
and that establishing biological relationships can become pressing when existing realizations of kinship, whether biological and/or cultural, are perhaps
perceived as less than entirely fulfilling.

There are no sites, whether freestanding blogs or those connected to any
of these services, devoted to the original, authentically Italian surname of my

direct paternal line or to the surnames of my other seven great-grandparents. A search for groups devoted to my paternal or maternal haplogroups or to Italian genetic ancestry in general turned up the Italy DNA Project, which contained an article on the U3 mtDNA haplogroup. However, the blog appeared not to have been updated since 2007. Sites dedicated to the U mtDNA haplogroup and the G Y-DNA haplogroup are too broad to generate usefully specific information or discussion on my family's particular affinities. The discussion groups associated with Family Tree DNA include those dealing with the major subclades associated with these haplotypes. However, interested parties must join these groups by uploading their relevant DNA data, and I could not find a clear indication of what content or other opportunities await.

"Any U3a's out there?" was the title of a discussion thread featuring my maternal haplotype on a forum attached to one of the other sites. Several of those with U3a and offshoot haplotypes replied, often mentioning places and surnames on their family tree with the apparent hope of making a match. However, since U3a is thousands of years old and representative of the maternal lineage, the possibility of making a connection based on a surname is remote. The diversity of locations did seem to be a point of interest and occasionally confusion. Germany, Russia, Switzerland, Hungary, and England as well as Italy, France, Palestine, and Iraq were mentioned, as was Jewish background. A thread devoted to the G haplogroup reflected in my father's Y-DNA also existed, and although there seemed to be no discussant with his specific haplotype or even its nearest root, there was much awareness of the fact that new offshoots of G were showing up every day.

On balance, the services, texts, and practices considered here may reproduce but seldom challenge essentialist notions of race. As Catherine Squires emphasizes, hybridity does not always undermine regimes of purity. Under certain conditions, hybridity can call into question essentialist assumptions. The research reflects that for those who overtly or inferentially base their identity in white and/or male supremacy and privilege, genetic ancestry can serve as another weapon in the arsenal. In particular, the use of genetic ancestry for racist, racializing purposes calls for additional counterhegemonic, informed, and sustained pushback. Scientists bear some responsibility to warn of genetic ancestry's true meaning, limits, excesses, and abuses. The analysis suggests that an emphasis on genetic kinship can undercut alternative definitions of family. This process can occur when treatments of genetic ancestry confuse genetic and cultural inheritance, as when *Finding Your Roots* (2016) considered whether LL Cool J's interest in boxing was biologically transmitted from his previously unknown progenitors. However, genetic and cultural inheritance can become detached because of political, religious, or other disassociations. Hegemonic gender regimes can also be supported by the communication and practices associated with genetic ancestry science, as when the paternal line haplogroup appears to stand in for the totality of one's genetic ancestry.

In the arenas of digital and social media, genetic ancestry sites and practices form contexts that "enable people to manage their identity performances and their relationships," thereby fashioning "unique communication environments" (Comunello xiii). The research suggests that Rainie and Wellman's prediction of networked individualism replacing "densely knit family" with "far-flung" connections must be amended when the goal of genealogy generally and genetic ancestry specifically is to supplement the "densely knit" with the "far-flung" (location 441). Family historians can negotiate more expansive (and permeable) definitions of family that nonetheless have immediate family at their core. Whether close or distant, these relations can include adoptive and other alternative versions of family as links in a cultural familial chain. Overall, however, as Rainie and Wellman acknowledge, the "changing social environment is adding to people's capacity and willingness to exploit more 'remote' relationships—in both the physical and emotional senses of the word" (locations 477–80).

These insights confer significance on genealogy blogs, such as those devoted to paternal- or maternal-line DNA haplogroups as well as other genealogically relevant social media. However, in "Remaking Time and Space," Kevin Meethan maintains that restrictive notions of national and subcultural identity and affinity are giving way to "newer, individualized forms of identity that cut across the established categories of culture and place" (99). This approach challenges Castells's view that in the new media environment, "the search for identity, ascribed or constructed, becomes the fundamental source of social meaning" (*Network Society* 3). Meethan concurs: the new situation is a double-edged sword since such individualized identity can also "facilitate reactionary and exclusionary politics," including those motivated by racism (99).

LOOSE ENDS, CONCLUSIONS, AND CRITICAL TRAJECTORIES

WRONG TURNS AND MISSING BRANCHES

Family historians are bound to have inaccurate or incomplete information in their family tree even before they hit that brick wall beyond which they cannot venture. Oversights may involve racial differences that are not recorded in documents or family narratives, but much missing information derives from adoption or mistaken paternity, gender identity, sexuality, ability, and/or class. These variables can intersect with race or help sustain racial hierarchies, as Patricia Hill Collins's research on intersectionality and the family structure suggests (see "All in the Family" 63).

One type of missing branch may have to do with adoption and/or other situations in which one or both of an individual's parents are believed or assumed to be biologically related but are not. Family history television, especially *Long Lost Family* (TLC, 2016–), has an automatic bias against known or newly revealed adoption and in favor of genetic kinship. Ironically, the one episode of the UK version of *Who Do You Think You Are?* (BBC, 2007) to trace an adoptive family tree profiled Nicky Campbell, a host of the UK version of *Long Lost Family* (ITV). A 2012 episode of *The Generations Project* (BYUtv), does focus on an adoptee, Ed, but he is mainly interested in establishing his *genetic* kinship to Native Americans through DNA testing. In a 2016 episode of *Genealogy Roadshow* (PBS), host/genealogist Joshua Taylor explains that he has a modern view of genealogy that allows for following adoptive lineages, and he does so in confirming a guest's connection to an individual charged in the Salem witch trials—the only time as of this writing that a US genealogy program has taken this route. Moreover, Internet searches for various combinations of the terms *adoption* or *adoptive* and *genealogy, ancestry, family tree,* or *family history,* result overwhelmingly in hits intended for adoptees attempting to identify their biological roots. Another group of sites present, among other things, designs for hard copy or digital family trees that record adoptive lineages. Blogs may take a more comprehensive accounting, sanctioning adoptive or "double" trees for adoptees but still stressing the importance of recording adoptive lineages *as such* and recommending resources that can help adoptees locate genetic kin (see Powell).

Oversights relating to adoption may also involve unrevealed adoptions, donor- or surrogate-assisted childbirth, and/or offspring via unacknowledged relationships. The young man who was DNA matched with me as a fifth cousin and desperate to identify his biological father illustrates the desire to make genetic connections as well as the difficulty that can be involved in doing so. In many instances, DNA testing and matching may produce a revelatory genetic link or anomaly, but more often or not, such breaks in the biological chain remain unresolved.

Preserving cultural definitions of kinship despite the pursuit of biological roots is not the only resistive imperative involved with adoption. Adoptions across racial or ethnic lines, especially those in which the apparent racial/ethnic background of an adoptee suggests marginal identity, can generate counterhegemonic impulses to establish and learn about the identities in question. Ed's story in *The Generations Project* is one such case. Adopted into a white Mormon family, Ed appeared to have Native American heritage, for which he displayed an urgent affinity, and he eventually confirmed his suspicions through engagement with Native Americans and DNA testing.

Similarly, the desire of descendants of African slaves to identify particular locations or tribes in Africa from their ancestors originated is a resistive inclination related to biological and cultural kinship. As discussed in the preceding chapter, Alondra Nelson's concept of affiliative self-fashioning clarifies this phenomenon, as does John L. Jackson's notion of racial sincerity. However, these tendencies do not apply solely to African Americans, particularly in the context of genetic ancestry.

Documents may occasionally hint at inconsistencies that involve ancillary relationships and/or unacknowledged offspring. My paternal grandmother's brother, Anthony, who attempted to prevent her and my grandfather from courting, was initially difficult to locate in the census and other available materials. I found a census record for a man with my great-uncle's name living with his wife, Emma, and naturalization records ultimately corroborated that this was indeed Uncle Tony. But Tony's wife was named Teresa. Letters between my grandparents allude to issues between Tony and Teresa even before they married, and their union apparently eroded long before they officially divorced late in life. In other sources, Tony lists himself as father to a boy who is unrecognized in other family documents. My family tree includes this child (about whom I have been able to find no further information), with a footnote indicating that Emma, not Teresa, may be his mother.

Most family tree software allows users to indicate both adoptive and biological parents and lineages. Family Tree Maker 2010, for instance, explains,

> The Preferred Parents dialog box lets you set up the default preferred relationship between parents and an individual. It presents a list of parents so you can select the couple to consider as "preferred." For example, if you are following the line of an adopted person, you have two lines you can follow, the biological line or the adoptive line. Depending on your intentions, you may want the biological parents to always be listed as the person's parents.

In this version of the software, having to select a "couple" as preferred seems to complicate the designation of biological parents, adoptive parents, and especially a biological and an adoptive parent who never married.

The Family Tree Maker 2010 software does not provide a straightforward way to record racial or ethnic identities or related distinctions within a family beyond relying on names and places of birth. Users would have to make special note of such information to ensure that it was carried forward within a family, and such notes might not appear in GEDCOM files made for easy dispersal.

A dearth of identified LGBT members in the family tree can constitute another problematic lapse. Family history television has profiled a number of gay or lesbian celebrities, among them tennis champion Billie Jean King (*Finding Your Roots*, 2014), rock musician Melissa Etheridge (*Who Do You Think You Are?*, 2015), actor/comic/talk-show host Rosie O'Donnell (*Who Do You Think You Are?*, 2011), journalist Anderson Cooper (*Finding Your Roots*, 2014), comic Wanda Sykes (*Finding Your Roots*, 2016), actors Jesse Tyler Ferguson (*Who Do You Think You Are?*, 2014) and Neil Patrick Harris (*Finding Your Roots*, 2016), and playwright/screenwriter Tony Kushner (*Finding Your Roots*, 2014). While LGBT persons are as interested in their family histories as straight and/or cisgender individuals, their status *within* a family history can be precarious. In "Hiding Out in the Open," Thomas MacEntee argues that identifying (with evidence) bygone LGBT family members is appropriate and historically significant, particularly in fleshing out family histories that go beyond simple pedigree. He goes on to suggest strategies such as becoming familiar with "coded" language that might appear in family artifacts, determining whether family members lived in known gay/lesbian neighborhoods, and observing their consistent travel or living partners. No identifications of bygone LGBT family members have as yet occurred on US genealogy series.

Many LGBT persons were unable to live their identities openly, and some became involved in heterosexual relationships. Family historians may have few avenues for identifying the sexual orientations and/or gender identities of such family members. However, genealogist Kim Cotton acknowledges the likelihood that LGBT branches on the family tree can reflect "'traditional' family structures" and that many include children, "even before adoption and surrogacy became feasible for same-sex couples."

Dealing straightforwardly with alternative means of *becoming* parents when creating a family tree is at least as difficult when the parents are in a same-sex relationship. For example, Cotton notes that only Mac Family Tree software allows parents to be designated as "partners." The recording of parental roles and alternative identities on family trees is even more problematic when a transgender individual is involved. In Julia Creet's documentary, *Need to Know: Ancestry and the Business of Family*, an Icelandic transgender woman explains that there is no consistency in how the *Íslendingabók* records parents like her. Some transgender women who genetically parent children are listed as fathers, while others are listed as second mothers. Will future versions of family tree software accommodate multiple configurations? When some stress "accuracy" above all else in genealogy, do they demand that only certain, prescribed options apply?

According to Cotton, many LGBT persons seek to "honor everyone" in the family tree and "let those later generations know that if they fall within the LGBT spectrum, they are not the first in the family." However, in this and many other situations, having children or being in the direct line of descent should not be prerequisites for integration into a full-fledged family history. After all, on *Family Tree* (HBO, 2013), Tom Chadwick's lesbian aunt bequeaths him the box of mementos that launches him on his genealogical journey.

Major wrong turns in my family history efforts involved my paternal grandmother's eldest sister, known by her middle name, Rosa. My father never knew his aunt. While we share ancestors, she is not in my direct line of descent. Yet her story enriches the family history by hinting at pressures affecting immigrants in the United States in the early twentieth century and conditions in the homeland that may have contributed to emigration. The tale of her life also foregrounds the significance of intersections involving race/ethnicity, gender, and class and demonstrates how genealogical misdirection can occur, obscuring significant, overarching contexts. In addition, it highlights the importance of including maiden names on censuses and other civil records. Embracing full-fledged *family history* as opposed to featuring only those in one's lines of descent in a straightforward *genealogy* creates such broader contexts and deepens one's critical perspective. It can do so in ways not depicted on family history television, where detours off the pedigree chiefly occur to account for renowned family members or events. Broadening one's scope also speaks to the "chasm" currently deliberated in genealogical circles, in which interpersonal and narrative aspects of family history confront digitally based genealogy focusing on pedigree alone (see "The Chasm").

As discussed in chapter 2, according to family lore, Rosa had died in the 1918–19 influenza pandemic, and we had assumed that she did not immigrate to the United States with the rest of her family because she was married by the time they embarked. Although I explored the possibility that she and her husband and children had indeed emigrated, doing so produced documentation suggesting that stories about her death were inaccurate, so I concluded that these documents referred to a different person.

When my sister and I visited the family's Calabrian hometown in 2014, we confirmed Rosa's married surname and obtained additional information showing that she emigrated. As a result, I returned home and reexamined an arrival document that I had previously dismissed as not representing Rosa's family because this family appeared intact in the 1930 US census. Having verified the names, the arrival document now appeared to match Rosa's family, and the census seemed to indicate that she had not died in the pandemic. However, although the 1920 census record for the family listed Rosa's husband, Domenico, as married, neither Rosa nor their daughter, Margherita, was listed as residing with the rest of the family. Deepening the mystery, a closer examination revealed that the name *Rosa* had apparently initially been included in the census but then rubbed out.

I continued to dig and found further documentation pertaining to the family. In 1914, Domenico had applied for a passport to take Rosa and their four children to Italy "for their health"; in 1919, he submitted another application to retrieve his children from Italy. The subsequent arrival document lists him and his three sons, but not Rosa or Margherita. Ten years later, Domenico finally accompanied a teenaged Margherita back from Italy. This information seemed to lend credence to the family lore that Rosa had died of the flu in Italy. But then why did she appear in the 1930 census? The death records for some of the family's children ultimately provided me with an answer: there were two different Rosas. After my great-aunt's death, Domenico married another woman who had the same name and was roughly the same age. Positive confirmation of my deduction that Rosa I died of the flu in late 1918 still awaits further research—perhaps another visit to the ancestral town and a stroll through the local cemetery.

The influenza pandemic hit extremely hard in Italy, where it was known as La Spagnola (the Spanish Flu) and peaked in October–November 1918 (Ansart et al.). Mortality rates across Europe were higher in countries with lower economic status—that is, primarily Southern European nations. And southern Italy's poverty relative to the northern part of the country might have rendered the region even more vulnerable.

Margherita's story, too, is quite illuminating. Although she was born and died in the United States, she apparently lived in her ancestral hometown during other phases of her life. A 1953 document records her return to the United States, potentially the occasion on which my father may have encountered her. Other questions arise: Why were Rosa and the children shipped off to Italy for four years shortly after Margherita's birth? Why did the girl not return to the States with her brothers? Did her father consider Italy a more wholesome environment for a girl, especially one whose ethnicity marginalized her in the new country? These questions reflect my own subjectivities and call for further investigation of conditions, customs, and values in the times and cultures in question.

It is also difficult to discover whether ancestors going back more than a couple of generations confronted physical, mental, and/or intellectual challenges unless those conditions are recollected in family lore and/or recorded in an unusual vital record. Moreover, my research by design highlights US television series, multicultural histories, and genealogical contexts. Many countries do not produce genealogy television series, and gaining access to such programs from other countries can be difficult, with linguistic barriers adding further hurdles to the analysis.

A search of Amazon.it, the Italian version of Amazon.com, revealed no DVDs directly pertaining to genealogy or family history. When I subscribed to Ancestry.com's World Explorer service, I discovered that Italian users appear more likely than their US counterparts to restrict access to their trees. Italians may consider family history a more personal activity. Britain's attention to multiculturalism in family history can be glimpsed by looking at its version of *Who Do You Think You Are?* (BBC2, BBC1 2004–).By 2015, the program had featured approximately sixteen profiles of celebrities whose heritage springs in whole or in part from outside Europe, mostly as a by-product of Britain's historical colonization of nations around the globe. However, these profiles are mostly front-loaded, with nine occurring between 2004 and 2008 (forty episodes) and seven occurring between 2009 and 2015 (seventy episodes). To what extent the episodes featuring these celebrities delve into non-European origins is undetermined. Among those of European background, central and northern locations predominate, with an unsurprising emphasis on the British Isles. Eastern Europe occasionally comes into play, especially when the program explores Jewish heritage. The US version of *Who Do You Think You Are?* (NBC; TLC) has thus far fared little better, but the PBS celebrity profile series have largely taken up the slack.

Like Bryan Sykes's *The Seven Daughters of Eve*, Debbie Kennett's *DNA and Social Networking: A Guide to Genealogy in the Twenty-First Century* addresses European and especially British readers. The book rarely mentions multicultural contexts. Her one-chapter discussion of autosomal DNA testing emphasizes its possibilities for matching within a national or regional context and relegates to afterthought an interest in determining multiple geographic affinities: "If you suspect that you have non-European ancestry, then the results could potentially be more revealing" (locations 2006–10). This bias is also evident as she reviews social networking sites related to genetic genealogy and DNA testing.

The American context offers convenient and fertile soil for critically exploring genealogy media and culture in terms of indigenous, colonized, and colonizing peoples; genocide by multiple means; patriarchy; slavery; segregation; colonial and postcolonial statuses; internment; racialization; racial and ethnic diversity; hybridity; immigration; and/or diasporic identity. It is not that other countries do not have similarly or even more multifaceted histories; rather, in the United States, these conditions have occurred recently enough for family historians to unearth and document their associations with at least *some* temporally proximate ancestors.

Ongoing migrations and influxes of refugees into European and other countries and the cultural controversies, insurgencies, and conflicts they stimulate could deepen and diversify investigatory climates related to family history media and culture in the digital age. Italy is one place where such developments bear watching. In 2013, Cecile Kyenge, an Italian citizen born in the Congo, stirred racist attitudes when she became the country's first black minister. She vowed to change current law to give citizenship to non-Italians born in Italy in a culture where "Italian nationality is passed on most commonly by blood" (Faris). Mario Borghezio, a European Parliament member representing Italy's Northern League, commented, "She seems like a great housekeeper . . . but not a government minister" (qtd. in Faris). Pino Aprile's *Terroni*, which chronicles the continuing marginalization of southern Italians and their internalization of such marginality, draws parallels between the racialized, anti-immigrant stance of many Northern League members and its desire to shortchange and in some quarters separate from the Mezzogiorno. Anti-immigrant sentiments have also arisen elsewhere in Italy, including in the central region of Lazio. The concierge at a Roman hotel warned us against going to a particular restaurant all because it was located near an immigrant enclave. I responded, "Tutti i miei bisnonni erano immigrati" (all my great-grandparents were immigrants), much to his confusion. Italy and other countries currently evolving along these lines are ripening for critical analysis of genealogy texts and practices. This volume provides approaches and guideposts for others to follow or amend as appropriate.

EXPANDING THE FIELD: DECIPHERING FAMILY HISTORIES AND MEMENTOS

Annette Kuhn's concept of *collective imagination* frames an approach to critically deconstructing family artifacts such as photos, documents, and letters that encourages links between personal memory and collective knowledge (165–66). This approach makes gathering keepsakes more than a routine exercise. I undertake this deconstruction by intertwining its four steps: (1) describing the artifact; (2) adopting the subjectivity of one or more persons depicted or referenced in it; (3) considering the contexts and technologies of production; and (4) situating its reception in the here and now (8). This application extends the approach to include and occasionally emphasize family history "facts" and narratives.

A photograph of my paternal grandmother, Giovannina/Genevieve (1906–70) with her family, ca. 1918, provides an apt example for analysis (see figure 7.1). I approximated the year of the photograph based on two aspects—my grandmother's apparent age and a comparison with dated photos of her, and the fact that her younger brother appears to be wearing a World War I–era US military uniform. The information I discovered about my grandmother's older sister, Rosa (1893–1918), who is not in the photograph, adds to the plausibility of that date and gives rise to a deeper, more complete analysis of the photo. Rosa's hypothesized death in Italy establishes an intersection with Armistice Day, 11 November 1918, the end of the First World War.

Figure 7.1: My paternal grandmother Giovannina/Genevieve (1906–70) (far right), with her family, New York, ca. 1918. Her parents, Maria (1869–1946) and Francesco/Frank (1860–1947), are seated in front, and the other children are (left to right) Luigi/Louis (1908–86), Giovanni/John (1903–?), Carolina/Kate (1900–1985), and Pasquale Antonio/Anthony (1898–1973).

In *Sleeping Beauty: Memorial Photography in America*, Stanley Burns notes that from 1910 through the 1930s, Victorian-era postmortem family photographs, which had often included the staged body of the deceased, gave way to focusing on steadfast survivors. Commemorating Rosa's death and the victory of the family's new homeland might well account for both the photographic occasion and the family's display of military and dark-hued bereavement attire, although the need for Italians, a marginalized, racialized, immigrant group, to overtly portray their loyalty and aspirational citizenship could also explain the military garb.

Giovannina's parents, Maria (1869–1946) and my second great-grandfather named Francesco/Frank (1860–1947), are seated front and center, presented as esteemed figures guiding their offspring. From a twenty-first-century perspective, the nine-year difference in their ages is not apparent. Their youngest children flank them—Luigi/Louis (1908–86) at left and my grandmother, who would have been about twelve, at right. Behind the younger children and in front of an ornate backdrop stand the older children: (left to right), Giovanni/John (1903–?), Carolina/Kate (1900–1985), and Pasquale Antonio/Anthony (1898–1973), who later interfered with my grandparents' courtship.

Aunt Kate subsequently became the mother of Dad's cousin, Bob, and a colorized photograph loaned to me by Bob and his wife shows Kate as a Red Cross nurse during the war era. Two of the three older children rest a hand on the back of a parental chair. John's jacket appears to feature some sort of military insignia, but only Anthony is old enough to have served, and I have found no evidence that he did.

All of the clothing is dark aside with the exceptions of the men's shirts, Louis's khaki uniform, the plaid in Grandma's dress, and the large white bow in her hair. The women's dresses are cinched at the waist, but Grandma's is shorter, exposing dark, calf-height socks. Frank wears a three-piece suit and like Antonio has a pin on the lapel. Maria's dress features a tie around its Chelsea collar, while Kate's dress is lower cut, and she and my grandmother sport floppy versions of the Chelsea known as the Dog Ear. John sports a double-breasted suit.

Photographic technology and portraiture style of the time begins to explain what today we would interpret as sad, sullen faces (see Jones) and possibly describe as "resting bitch face." In that era, having a photographic portrait taken was expensive and still relatively rare, especially for a poor, immigrant family. The only comparison many people could make at that time was to painted portraits, which traditionally depicted subjects in a state of heightened dignity. Technologically speaking, keeping still was a necessity because of the slower shutter speeds of cameras, and remaining still is much easier with resting facial muscles than when smiling. Solemnity is thus a common feature of old photographic portraits. However, in some cases, including this one, those depicted might well have good reason to look glum.

At the time the photo was taken, my grandmother, might have keenly felt the pressures of navigating between two cultures. She arrived in the United States in 1912, at the age of six and, would have had five or six years of schooling by this time, effectively making her bilingual. Her version of English was a broken Brooklynese, but her parents (and almost certainly her deceased sister) would not have been able to speak it with her. Genevieve/Giovannina was two when Rosa married and thus could not have recalled growing up alongside her. Her sister's story might have been a cautionary tale. At some point that I have been unable to determine, my grandmother learned to read and write in the standard Italian that occasionally appears in the letters she exchanged with my grandfather. Her parents and other elder family members spoke in dialect and could not read or write, and the public school system was not likely responsible; church and/or after-school programs remain a possibility.

On the verge of a new age, Genevieve/Giovannina might have curbed her sadness with hope. She could not have known that she would marry in 1924 and that just prior to her twentieth birthday, she would give birth to her eldest child, my father. She also could not have known that she and her husband would struggle to raise him and his younger brother through the Great Depression and that both sons would fight in a second world war while their little sister toddled at home. Nor would she have predicted that both she and her daughter would die of cancer in their mid-sixties which, at the time of my grandmother's death, I naively believed would cease to be a threat by the time I was her age. Although I was no longer a child when Grandma died, I could not bear to look at her in her casket: I did not want to remember her that way. She had occasionally entertained neighborhood children, most of them Jewish, with playing cards and spaghetti, and they attended the funeral. However, as I later recognized, Grandma was only one of my grandparents who had difficulty accepting other varieties of racial/ethnic difference.

As the photo was taken, Giovannina/Genevieve's mother, born Maria Orrico in the Cosenza province of Calabria, near the town where she later lived and where her six children were born, might have felt regret that she and her family could not provide a haven for Rosa and her offspring when, for whatever reason, the situation demanded it. Perhaps she also regretted allowing Rosa to marry at age fifteen. Rosa, herself barely grown, gave birth to four children over the next ten years and then succumbed to La Spagnola, leaving them to navigate life without her. Maria might be imagining her daughter sick and alone and reflecting on her own life and youth, calculating the toll taken by giving birth to six children, laboring in the fields to feed them, and worrying about them throughout *la miseria*. As a poor nineteenth-century *contadina* from a deeply devout and socially conservative culture, what other course could she have taken? The physical and cultural upheaval of migration and the continuing struggle as immigrants in the new land might have also weighed heavily on her mind. Maria died in 1946, a year before her husband. My father, still serving in the US army in occupied Austria, did not get to say good-bye to her.

Applying Kuhn's strategy even in the absence of densely meaningful artifacts is also possible if genealogical information, personal study and observation, and interpersonal narratives make up the slack. Maria and my other great-grandmothers (see figure 7.3) were marginalized by identities of gender, class, race/ethnicity, and/or age, but they have offered an opportunity to give voice to the voiceless and compare and contrast their stories with

Figure 7.2: My great-grandmothers (left to right), Maria Orrico (1869–1946), Elisabetta Campanella (1862–1924), Cristina Zito (1871–1941), and Adelina DeMaddi (1871–1905).

those of others according to developing and ongoing issues of power. All of them died before their husbands and at considerably younger ages; their husbands were between eleven and thirty-five years older when they died. Each of my great-grandmothers gave birth to between six and eight children. All were impoverished, racialized, southern Italian females and consequently considered by those of privilege on both sides of the Atlantic to be on the lower rungs of the social ladder.

The correlation between poverty and lowered life expectancy is well established. Not only does Séverine Ansart et al.'s study of the influenza pandemic suggest the greater vulnerability of poorer, southern populations, but poverty continues to decrease longevity (Lowry), and this effect can be even greater for women (Weldon). Having fewer children has also been associated with exceptional longevity for both men and women in some populations (Tabatabaie et al.), while other research has found that lower levels of reproduction contribute to increasing life expectancies among women ("Fewer Children").

Elisabetta Campanella (1862–1924), my paternal-line great-grandmother, was born in Calabria, at the very bottom of Italy's boot, in the southernmost province of the southernmost region of the Italian peninsula. Here, coastal waterways for millennia facilitated the migration of peoples from three continents and from what we would now consider to be three different races. Assumptions concerning this history and geography have helped enable the racialization of southern Italians. The men in her family and her husband's families tilled the soil and herded cattle, which might account for photos of my grandfather on horseback and my father's cultural affinity for Westerns. By the same token, the seaside locale might have influenced my family's cultural preferences regarding homesteads and/or vacation locales. Elisabetta herself was a spinner of yarn. Her husband, Nicola Scuteri (1854–1935), preceded her and their son to America by two years, in keeping with a common pattern among Italian immigrants (Mangione and Morreale). She, like many other women left behind—including Maria Orrico—might have wondered about the integrity of her marriage during the separation. Elisabetta gave birth to seven children, one of whom died in childhood. In 1924, at the age of sixty-one, she succumbed to complications of flu and pneumonia, a fate reminiscent of my father's maternal Aunt Rosa. The following year, my father was born.

Cristina Zito (1871–1941), my mother's maternal grandmother and my namesake, was born in the Salerno province of Campania, not far from Naples. Her husband, Antonio (1871–1955), married her on one of several trips back to his hometown from the United States, where he eventually built a career working for steamship lines. After their wedding, he headed back to the United States without her. Shortly thereafter, he (almost certainly) decided to migrate permanently, and Cristina was four months pregnant with my grandmother while making the crossing on her own. According to my mother, Cristina was a great cook: "She just smelled the ingredients and put things together." The only recipe passed down to my mother was for *struffoli*, Neapolitan fried-dough Christmas cookies that were shaped into trees and covered with honey and sprinkles. (My siblings and I thought that they were fun to make and look at but not nearly as enjoyable to eat.) Cristina bore seven daughters and one son. This branch seems to have been the primary contributor of my family's affinity for music, as at least three of Cristina's daughters, including my grandmother, were proficient at the piano. For stretches in their lives, several of my grandmother's sisters appear to have worked outside the home and/or not had husbands in attendance. My grandmother had five children, but none of her sisters had more than two, and some had none. Two of the sisters lived to be just shy of one hundred, and four of the remaining five made it well into their eighties or early nineties. Those born in the twentieth century seem particularly to epitomize the changing parameters for women. Cristina died at the age of sixty-nine of sudden-onset diabetes, fourteen years before her husband. According to a family story, she was buried with pomp and circumstance in the robes of a lay order to which she belonged.

The romance between my mother's paternal grandmother, Maria Adelina DeMaddi (1871–1905), and grandfather, Francesco Paolo (1866–1935), was about as star-crossed as real love stories can get. It unfolded in a town in the Cosenza province of Calabria, not far from the birthplace of my maternal grandmother. Adelina's experience perhaps most reflects divisions of gender, race, and class in the cultures in which she and my other great-grandmothers lived. I often wonder when she began imagining that she might become part of the well-heeled family for which her family worked. After she and the family's eldest son fell in love, when did she learn of his father's objections? Would she have overheard the conflict ignited by Francesco's desire to marry her? Might she have doubted her own worthiness? After all, Francesco's mother was a noblewoman, and his grandfather had died a hero, defending Italian unification. But unification had failed to offer those of *her* class and racialized status—*contadini*, spinners, and bricklayers—a better life. Because of its durable intersection with whiteness, the elevated class status of Francesco's family likely superseded the racialization that otherwise accompanies a southern background. When his father disowned Francesco for marrying her, a terrible weight likely fell squarely on Adelina's shoulders. I have not located their marriage document: the influence of Francesco's father probably meant that they married somewhere else, and I have not yet discovered where.

Despite Francesco's education, their migration to the United States did not appreciably improve their situation. My grandfather, their third child, was born six months after their arrival. Francesco found work in New York's garment industry but never learned enough English to advance much beyond his position as a presser. Although her brother and sister had also migrated and her mother had joined their new adventure, Adelina still took her children back to Italy in 1903 and there gave birth to her sixth and final child. Two years later, at age thirty-four, she died of uterine cancer. Her death occurred in Manhattan, although the family lived in Brooklyn. Perhaps her deathbed was located at her brother's or sister's house, with her mother caring for her (mostly?) unsuspecting children in Brooklyn. Adelina's death might have played some role in causing Francesco's depression or other condition that led to his stint in a sanitarium, but he recovered and outlived his wife by another thirty years, dying at age sixty-nine.

FINDINGS AND STRATEGIES

This study's overarching goal has been to gauge the extent to which genealogical practitioners, practices, institutions, tools, and texts mobilize critical postures and objectives, particularly regarding race and ethnicity, and determine how practitioners might increase their attention to such a critical orientation. As the components of this question are separated and explored, critical trajectories for addressing lapses emerge. One secondary issue concerns whether the components of family history media and culture produce *critical* negotiations of individual identity, connections between the individual and the collective historical, and/or connections between historical and contemporary struggles. Analysis of family history television has revealed that drawing connections between a profiled individual and historical events is chief among the genre's goals but that inaccurate or incomplete information is at times provided, in part because shows focus too much on the individual and fail to highlight how his/her family might be atypical of broader historical issues and patterns.

On *African American Lives* (2006) and *African American Lives 2* (2008), revelations that a profiled celebrity's female slave ancestor likely had a consenting, mutually desired postemancipation relationship with her former holder might allow this celebrity to breathe a sigh of relief but in the absence of broader context can create the impression that unions were common. The selection of celebrities is crucial if the narrative and other elements suggest that their family histories are representative of groups to which they belong. However, name recognition, availability, and other factors appear to drive this choice. Certainly, the selection of Mario Batali to represent Italian newcomers during the Century of Immigration likely created a false impression that the people chose to leave for vague or indeterminate reasons and that most immigrants did not come from a geographically specific, impoverished, racialized, and politically exploited group.

Conversely, family history media—not only television shows but also online archives and genealogy websites—miss dozens of opportunities to draw parallels between the past and present. Three discoveries in my family's immigration history presented clear connections with ongoing controversies. First, when I found that two of my grandparents were born in the United States but conceived in Italy, it struck me that today they would qualify as "anchor babies" and have their native citizenship challenged in certain quarters. Second, my study of the Italian diaspora confirmed that most Italian migrants, including all four of my great-grandfathers, did not initially journey here intending to stay but instead sought to make money to support their families back home (though they may also have been testing out the idea of permanently emigrating) (see Mangione and Morreale). Many Italians worked in the United States but then returned to their homeland. Third, I confirmed that most of my immigrant ancestors over a certain age never learned English. All three of these phenomena—not intending to become citizens, not quickly learning English, and arriving with a child in utero who would then acquire birthright citizenship—make their way into nativist arguments against today's newcomers, as natives spuriously contrast the contexts of the recent migrations with those of earlier migrants.

The quarantine incident involving the ship on which one of my great-grandfathers arrived also suggests that legal entry does not circumvent such nativist objections. By uncovering public resistance to legal immigration and learning that policies such as the Johnson-Reed Act were efforts to rescind earlier legalities in response to racism and nativism, genealogy practitioners might affirm, as I have, that such prejudices persist as motivators of anti-immigrant sentiment. Television profiles surely have missed opportunities to point out similar situations, and a lack of attention to the history of immigration restrictions in response to nativism compounds the oversight. Online affordances certainly could help users put documents and their information into the appropriate historical context of immigration, racism, and nativism and aid users in identifying relevant policies as well as similarities and differences between groups and eras.

A second subsidiary research question asks whether hybridity counter-hegemonically destabilizes identity in family history media and culture and whether such media and culture are sensitive to issues that arise when two or more aspects of identity intersect. Racist or racializing uses of hybridity might be a hegemonic outcome. In YouTube videos, for example, the genetic hybridity of Italians became a cudgel in the hands of those with racist motivations. A need to uphold one's cultural identity can also stand in the way of hybridity's potential to break down racial categories. The existence of hybridity had little validity for the lives of African Americans whom the one-drop rule classified as black even if their background was mostly white. Although many of the family history programs reflect the intersection of class and race, for example, they do not explicitly point out this connection. Host Henry Louis Gates Jr. fails to recognize revelatory intersections between race and gender. In fact, intersections between gender and other identities are seldom fodder for commentary in family history texts and practices, a lacuna that I begin to fill by gauging the intersections among gender, race, class, age, and nation in the lives of my immigrant great-grandmothers.

As for the third subordinate interrogatory—Does family history culture reproduce postidentity orientations?—the answer is *mostly* yes. By profiling celebrities, family history television automatically foregrounds those who appear to have overcome bigotry and struggle and suggests that doing so is the rule rather than the exception. Individual narratives in programs that do not profile celebrities, such as BYUtv's *The Generations Project*, gesture in the direction of simply forgiving and forgetting past injustices. A countervailing

prospect emerges through observing others as they discover previously unknown injustices or dimensions of injustice. Even if a profiled celebrity seems
to have transcended the past, her/his learning about previously unrecognized
struggles might encourage audience members to deepen their knowledge in
a manner that unearths parallels with ongoing issues and circumstances. As
I learned more about my *southern* Italian and Italian American roots, this
is precisely what occurred. However, increasing the likelihood of such an
outcome is more difficult.

Fourth, do discourses and practices specific to genetic ancestry privilege
ethnocentricity, patrilineal connections, and genetic rather than cultural
notions of kinship, and do they provide cover or grist for essentialist, racist,
and/or racializing rhetoric? The evidence here indicates that uses of genetic
ancestry science in family history texts and practices tend to uphold genetic
definitions of kinship. Television's lack of attention to adoptive lineages and
celebratory portrayal of DNA testing as well as the marketing and advertising
of testing services represent genetic kinship as indispensable and preemi-
nent. But despite genetics, I share little affinity with the 2X great-grandfather
who disowned his son or with my grandmother's brother who attempted to
prevent her from marrying my grandfather.

Those engaged in racist, racializing, and ethnocentric endeavors often
distort genetic ancestry science to buttress their arguments. Because testing
services and other media depictions use the term *ethnic ancestry* or otherwise misrepresent the science, fail to warn against these misuses, and/or
fail to assert that racial categories are socially constructed, such endeavors
often remain insufficiently challenged. Patrilineal thinking also dominates
in texts and practices of genealogy and genetic ancestry because Y-DNA is
the primary mechanism for determining human migration patterns, because
patrilineal naming gives rise to "surname studies" and makes researching
maternal lineages more difficult, and because historical efforts to record
genealogical information often favored paternal lineages that determined
inheritance and/or descent from a ruling clan. This has led to the (possibly
incorrect) identification of a Y-DNA haplogroup being used to declare, for
example, that King Tutankhamen must have been European even though
this haplogroup represents only one of his multitudinous lineages. Wrong
turns in family history, such as my misdirected conclusion that my father's
Aunt Rosa did not die in the influenza pandemic of 1918–19, occur because
maiden names are not always evident in vital records.

Fifth, how do the enterprises and institutions of family history threaten privacy and inflect issues relating to economics, marketing, and cross-marketing

of relevant media and services. The 1990 founding of Ancestry.com as a consequence of the distribution of LDS genealogical data was one of the early signs of cooperation for mutual benefit among institutions of family history culture. A collaboration between deCODE Genetics and the person who first digitized Iceland's *Íslendingabók* family genealogies appropriated and continued these genealogies for use, along with citizens' health records, for genetic research without informed consent until the courts intervened (Creet). Ancestry.com's sponsorship of family history television has resulted in seamless integration of the website into program narratives. The additional use and promotion of genetic ancestry testing services in such narratives in exchange for onsite advertising of the programs and other compensation has also become routine in the cross-pollination and interweaving of various institutions involved in family history culture.

The legal issues regarding lack of consent and/or data mining that have affected deCODE Genetics and 23andMe reveal that privacy rights are legitimate ongoing concerns extending into the arena of race and ethnicity in that genetic propensities for some diseases can be identified among particular racial and/or ethnic groups. Might employers require potential employees to provide health information from DNA testing as a condition of employment? Ancestry.com's decision to discontinue its integrated software, Family Tree Maker, will undoubtedly encourage more consumers to depend solely on Ancestry.com's family tree application, with only a difficult transition to new software allowing them to maintain these records privately and independently. The process is also likely to increase paid subscriptions to Ancestry.com's database services. Moreover, as genealogical database services and genetic ancestry testing services align with family history television, genetic definitions of kinship are likely to become even more prevalent in all such texts and services.

A sixth pivotal query involves the media landscape on which family history texts, practices, and institutions currently function. What might we learn about convergent, digital, and social media and the social relations by which they operate by interrogating their function and role in this context? Elisa Giaccardi provides a helpful analytical framework involving three dimensions: (1) *social practice*, or "understanding and experiencing heritage" by way of "novel social practices of collection, representation, and communication enabled and promoted by social media"; (2) *public formation*, or the "presence of widely available social technologies" stimulating "peer-to-peer activities such as information and media sharing"; and (3) *sense of place*, in which "social media and technologies support new ways to engage with

people, interpretations, and values that pertain to a specific territorial setting" (locations 4–14).

Given that networked individualism, in Barry Wellman's terms, disrupts
more stable understandings of kinship in that "people often have complex
household relations, with stepchildren, ex-marital partners (and their progeny), and multiple sets of in-laws" ("Little Boxes" 10) and that this complexity might involve racial variance, tight-knit notions of family recede. The
impetus to research one's biological and/or corresponding cultural roots is
then recalibrated accordingly. However, this analysis has uncovered ways in
which a lack of family cohesion can also give rise to a search for what and
Lee Rainie and Barry Wellman refer to as "far-flung" relations (location 441),
as when my fifth cousin reached out to me for possible information on his
biological father. Such peer-to-peer communications using social media are
characteristic of a public formation. A contestant on *Relative Race* (BYUtv,
2016–) is motivated to participate in a competition that involves uniting
competitors with unknown family members because her immediate family
is not close. Here, the person has bypassed the digitized public formations
in which the program itself has engaged to make connections with remote
family members. I built my family tree using online databases, interpersonal
information, and traditional and digital social media to connect with aunts
and uncles as well as close and distant cousins in the United States, Italy,
and elsewhere. A phone conversation with my father's cousin coupled with
a social media connection (via Ancestry.com) with a previously unknown
second cousin and cooperative research involving the two of us enabled
identification of the town in Calabria from which our paternal lineage comes.
Again, interpersonal information combined with a public formation in which
digital databases and social media interaction yielded results.

While none of these examples challenges the primacy of genetic kinship,
recognizing that *cultural* familial connections play a role in motivating one to
engage in family history also creates the potential to recognize and stimulate
new versions of family. Although political and religious differences resurfaced
when I connected on Facebook with my maternal cousins Facebook, the
cousins' culturally bequeathed engagements with music remained. What *is*
knowable through my family history research, (digital and traditional) social
media interaction, and other interpersonal practices is that my grandmother
and a couple of her sisters played the piano, and my grandfather played the
violin. My mother majored in music in college, and she and her sister were
avocational and sometimes professional musicians. Critical engagements
with and/or proficiencies in music evident in a significant number of their

children, nieces, and nephews have been recognized on social media. My cousins on this side of the family recently engaged in a vigorous Facebook discussion about the vocal performances in the 2012 movie version of *Les Miserables*. One of the Italian second cousins whom I first contacted on Facebook along with his brother had been a musician, suggesting that this cultural bequest has an even longer history. Recognizing or revisiting political and religious differences within the extended family relates to a sense of place. Debates on social media involved, among other things, the 2012 and 2016 presidential elections in the United States, and social media posts by an Italian relation regarding the latter contest were addressed to his compatriots but attracted the participation of Italian American kin. The varying viewpoints were clearly conditioned by place.

The array of cousins on the other side of my family consists only of the two adopted children of my father's younger sister, with whom I also interact on social media. I strive to be considerate of when and how I might interest them in my genealogical journey and its outcomes, particularly with regard to genetic ancestry. In fact, one of them was concerned about genetic risks when planning a family but found that his adoption records had been compromised. The other has recently met her genetic family. Even in terms of conventional genealogy, I would like to provide them with a special version of the family history album I am compiling that includes information, documents, and images related to their mother's family tree gleaned from social practices utilizing interpersonal and digital media. This album, which would emphasize cultural heritage, could be distributed in digital format. One thing is certain: for the better part of my siblings' and my lives, these have been our closest cousins. Cultural family ties, it seems, can forge a bond that is thicker than blood. A step beyond such a realization is understanding that nongenetic affinities can create familial relationships, even outside the bonds of marriage or adoption. Social media's facility in connecting far-flung individuals contributes to such understandings.

Given that networked individualism appears to elevate the singular person rather than the collective, media applied to genealogical practice can enable and/or hinder the ability to counterhegemonically parlay interpretations and realizations of kinship into a historically collective and ultimately contemporarily critical perspective that mobilizes senses of place. These conclusions have already addressed how television series, online databases, and genetic ancestry services might resist hegemony by avoiding post- orientations, digging for political and economic contexts for migration and protest, and linking individual to group histories and group histories to one another.

Finally, with respect to digital and traditional media, it is important to consider how the supposed chasm in genealogy might be negotiated in light of networked individualism and the critical questions of this study. If the primary motivation for engaging in genealogy is the immediate family, then networked individualism might discourage such engagement. However, once a person commits to the practice, networked individualism's broader scope would not only enhance the ability to accurately fulfill genealogical requirements but encourage one to venture beyond pedigree and digitally acquired "facts." Interpersonal narratives that emanate from a wider array of sources are likely to deepen connections and perspectives in ways that characterize post-chasm family history. Pursuing Aunt Rosa's story was an exercise in post-chasm family history that facilitated critical comprehension of the diasporic predispositions and experiences of southern Italian immigrants in the United States. However, the story benefited from the convenience of digital archives. The chasm metaphor, which reflects an either/or proposition, is consequently ill-fitting.

In July 2015, two of my maternal cousins organized the Mile High Big Italian Cousins Reunion near Denver, where their families had migrated decades earlier. The reunion was arranged partly via Facebook, and family photos, information, and reminiscences were shared via social media, eventually on a special page devoted to branches of the family. This sharing continued at the reunion, where I met the sister of one of the two second cousins killed on 11 September 2001. I had already encountered her first cousin through DNA matching and email. Several cousins huddled over a large map of Italy and circled the ancestral locations in the Mezzogiorno. We watched home movies that brought the recently bereaved to tears and played a game in which younger attendees were asked to identify others based on biographical factoids such as the latest family member to climb Mount Kilimanjaro and the family member who is a university professor. A number of the more than seventy attendees were related to my father as well as my mother—four of were my first cousins on my mother's side and second cousins on my father's. However, the insularity that may have contributed to three marriages between the same two families was not evident in any other respect. Italian, yes, but in-laws and descendants of Irish, Polish, Jewish, Latina/o, Asian, African American, and other backgrounds were present or acknowledged, something my grandparents could not have imagined.

Following the reunion, new relations continued to assemble on the family Facebook page. The introduction of a sister of the other second cousin (this time, once removed) who lost her life on 9/11 confirmed my deductions

Figure 7.3: Dad (right) and his cousin, Bob, during their final visit, 2010.

about where that branch fit on the family tree. At about the same time, a Spanish-speaking relative from Argentina announced her presence on the family page. I had noted Argentinians on Facebook with my mother's distinctive paternal family name, which originates with a single family in a single town in Italy. Spaniards and Brazilians with this name were similarly in evidence, and face-to-face genealogical research in Italy confirmed that cousins along my mother's maternal lineage had migrated to Brazil. Using Facebook's translation feature, we eventually established that the paternal uncle of my mother's paternal grandfather had founded the Argentinian branch of the family along with his wife. Translating given names became a sticking point that necessitated explanation across the cultural and language barrier—for example, in clarifying that an Italian immigrant known as José in Argentina would have started life as Giuseppe.

The sixteen months leading up to the cousins' reunion was also a time of loss, as Aunt Evelyn, Uncle David, cousin Massimo (whom I met in in Italy), and my dearest dad all passed on. After he died, my assigned task was to notify his cousins. Cousin Bob had called Dad the previous Christmas, but Dad no longer remembered him. When I went online to verify Bob's phone number, I instead found his obituary. He had died two days before my father. The waterworks started up again but, despite my tears, I was comforted by the fact that in 2010 we had taken the trip that united the two cousins one last time (see figure 7.3).

Using critical, "alternate roots" genealogy, I recuperated my ethnic identity by deepening my knowledge of the struggles that shaped my progenitors and by proactively relating their experience to and distinguishing it from that of other cultural groups. In this context, the expression *recuperating ethnic identity* has two meanings: (1) acquiring new information and insights concerning one's own racial/ethnic background that illuminate previous and ongoing struggles, and (2) interrogating one's racial/ethnic identifications, uncovering contextual correspondences with and departures from other groups, and cultivating understanding of their historical and/or current circumstances. While a critical genealogy requires both recuperations, those who currently navigate racial/ethnic minority status engage in the first recuperation daily. For others of multiple and/or unidentified ethnicities and/or those whose ethnic background does not require sustained negotiation, this recuperation requires new or renewed effort. However, the second recuperation demands such effort of all participants in genealogy culture.

Several strategies aid in such recuperation. *Understanding race constructively and consequentially* alludes to conceiving racial categories as social constructions that nevertheless have devastating effects. Minimizing structural, material, and immediate urgencies can impair a social constructionist perspective, as Eric King Watts indicates. However, it is plausible to hold a social-constructionist view while demonstrating, as I endeavor to do in my teaching, that social constructions have consequences, which may be different in kind, duration, and degree based on the group in question. I explain to students that this is why I have lived with the privilege of a white Italian American, unlike the majority of my southern Italian progenitors. I add that inhabitants of the United States might consider Jorge Mario Bergoglio, who became Pope Francis, to have been a racially unprivileged Latin American from Argentina, while his family's northern Italian homeland conferred racial privilege on his ancestors. Given such examples, students interpret racial classifications as neither biological nor fixed. As long as *me-too-ism* and especially *me-and-not-them-ism* are avoided and the consequences, structural exigencies, and racialization processes associated with different racial categories are addressed, this approach facilitates students' understanding of their own family histories and struggles as well as those of others. Changing demographics suggesting that whites will be a minority in the United States by 2043 (Kayne) present the possibility that new or shifting racial categories might emerge even as some racial categories remain durable and persistent. Moreover, anyone, living, working, and/or studying in a new cultural environment can be befuddled by local understandings of racial classifications. Both situations require recognizing racialization as it may operate to reshuffle previously assumed racial categories so that the motivations behind and potential consequences of the creation of a given racial regime can be properly interrogated. However, addressing the negative material effects and structural racism affecting those of temporally and geographically immediate racial minority groups should also be prioritized.

The online discussion regarding color differences between northern and southern Italians in the wake of the Batali profile on *Faces of America* (2010) reveals the significance of the north/south divide as well as race-based colorism *within* a racial category, another phenomenon that involves racialization and informs the critical chronicling of family history. In an episode of *Finding Your Roots* (2012), Latina actor Michelle Rodriguez and Latina political commentator Linda Chavez confront peculiar branches in their family trees reflective of the intermarriage of cousins motivated by race-based colorism designed to enhance "European" heredity. Bringing colorism to light in various genealogy texts and practices can diminish postracial claims of color blindness. It is one of the reasons that today, when someone wonders where my family comes from, I answer without hesitation, "*Southern* Italy." Like actor Don Cheadle, I believe that you are what you have to defend.

A second strategy entails *contemplating immigration and diaspora.* The three critical facts I discovered about my ancestors' immigration illustrate how digging into one's family history can help create an empathetic context for negotiating contemporary circumstances. Some immigration critics assert the legality of earlier immigration to differentiate it from current arrivals. Uncovering public resistance to earlier, legal immigration and learning that policies such as the Johnson-Reed Act sought to compromise this legality in response to racism and nativism suggest that the legality issue does not drive nativist proclivities. Such conclusions can be brought to light by providing the option—for example, in a pop-up window when someone searches immigration records on a genealogy website—to compare and contrast the policies and politics conditioning the immigration of certain groups in certain eras. Doing so would reveal correspondences and distinctions in public opinion and policy in various circumstances. Family history television, too, has thus far been derelict in noting how immigration restrictions such as those contained in the Johnson-Reed and Chinese Exclusion Acts targeted particular groups along racial and/or ethnic lines.

A third strategy implicates DNA testing for "ethnic ancestry" and involves *putting the genes in their place.* The explanation of autosomal testing found on the website of the Genographic Project declares, "You will also receive a visual percentage breakdown of your genomic ancestry by regional genetic affiliation. . . . Your regional genetic affiliations reflect the ancient migratory paths of your ancestors." Without profit as its impetus, the project can avoid problematic terms such as *ethnic ancestry* and instead speak of "affiliation" with migratory groups. The label on the largest slice of the pie chart the project produced for me is "Mediterranean," which includes slivers of three continents and consequently is not easily reducible to a racial category. The project might extend its caution and address potential abuses of this science, as Catherine Nash urges in "Genetic Kinship," but genealogy television and other services could similarly shift *their* language, illustrate racist abuses, and emphasize that all human DNA is 99.9 percent identical (Koenig, Lee, and Richardson 1). Two exigencies may inhibit these texts from doing so. One is that DNA supplies the only means of linking the progeny of African slaves to African tribes and locations, offering a keener sense of *African* identity than was previously possible—a major selling point. However, as Nash argues, "Many arguments for the value of . . . geneticised genealogy not only claim that they undermine race, but utilize the histories of violence, enslavement, and cultural dislocation to promote their potential to offer lost knowledge of origins and to make connections" ("Mapping Origins" 97). Second is the prevalence of cross-promotion, with family history series utilizing DNA and other services by name in exchange for advertising revenue or "corporate sponsorship."

Embracing cultural kinship, as did the poster on Television without Pity who stated that she was "Black because of a culture and a common struggle" of her forebears, also mitigates against definitions of family that are too bound up in genetics. When I reconnected with far-flung maternal cousins on social media, differing political views and understandings resurfaced, but multigenerational engagement with and/or expertise in music remained. Both of these are cultural, not genetic, bequests. In addition, my paternal cousins *by adoption* are closest to my siblings and me. Moreover, the recent family reunion verified that bonds of kinship are—appropriately—more adaptable than my very Italian grandparents would have reflected, as adoptees and family of an array of races and ethnicities were acknowledged.

Kramer's dictum that kinship can be reinforced *or* challenged through genealogy is commonsensical; consequently, both *acknowledging and disavowing* some ancestral relations is often appropriate. On *Who Do You Think You Are?* (NBC), actor Martin Sheen rejects a progenitor whose prejudice caused pain to others, including another ancestor on a different branch of his tree. While I cannot erase him from my family tree, I disavow my 2X great-grandfather whose class privilege led him to kick my great-grandfather out of the family.

Rather than getting the segment cut from his episode of *Finding Your Roots* (2014), Ben Affleck might have acknowledged and disavowed his slave-owning ancestor, as other guests have done. In the 2016 season of this series, white actor Ty Burrell learns about black female forebears *and* the white ancestor who impregnated one of them by slave rape. Perhaps with the Affleck incident in mind, Burrell responds, "There is no way to just separate [the white rapist] from the part I want to embrace. I want to just be with the heroines of the story." However, the most intriguing response to discovery of a slave-owning ancestor is actor Bill Paxton's on *Who Do You Think You Are?* (2015). With the aid of a genealogist, Paxton takes a detour to search for an unrelated slave named in his ancestor's will, locating the former slave on a census of free citizens. Genealogists and websites can develop digital and other tools that would encourage patrons to take such oppositional steps or even provide an automatic option to view a document recording a former slave listed in a will or similar record as a free citizen. However, such options should also refuse knee-jerk post- orientations and set a trajectory for deeper learning.

Alas, some family historians will not be guided by such illuminating strategies, and even those who are may fail to be enlightened. Many Irish, Italian, and other white ethnic Americans insist that the "golden door" of immigration be closed behind them because their ancestors did things the "right way," unlike those who followed. Such attitudes relate to race and, yes, to shifting racial categories. In fact, earlier immigrants felt the same way about Italian newcomers, as depicted in an 8 April 2017 *Saturday Night Live* sketch in which visitors to New York's Tenement Museum are entertained by actors portraying Polish migrants who blame their enduring struggles on recently arrived "greasy Italians."

Blogger Lachrista Greco recounts how her Calabrian grandfather's racism, especially against blacks, was motivated by his need to disown the internalized "African" descriptor used by northern Italians to demean southerners (a descriptor reproduced in the epithet *Guinea* leveled against Italian Americans). Greco also cites Jennifer Guglielmo and Salvatore Salerno's book, *Are Italians White?*, which quotes African American deejay Chuck Nice's commentary that "Italians are niggaz with short memories" (1). Guglielmo and Salerno contend that Nice was "calling Italians out on their particular whiteness," adding that Italians and many other ethnic Europeans "were not

Figure 7.4: Special effects, midcentury style. My father foreshadowed my interest in television by literally pasting a photo of me onto a photo of Mom leaning against the blank TV and then snapping this picture.

always white" and that the "loss of this memory is one of the tragedies of racism in America" (1).

Greco's ruminations reflect contextual understanding but not acceptance of the racism enacted by family elders. For deep-seated reasons, empathy has in some cases been scrupulously resisted. Rather than reasoning that you are what you have to defend, the inclination is to shun that identity. When the concierge at our Roman hotel reacted with deafening silence to the information that the next stop on our trip was my ancestral region, Calabria, I was momentarily jolted out of my assumptions of white privilege and in the long term identified more strongly as a southerner.

On 9 September 1950, the son of a working-class New York City Transit mechanic and a woman who took in sewing, a man who had accumulated college credits courtesy of the GI bill, married the middle-class, college-educated daughter of an accountant and a homemaker. They went on to produce my siblings and me. Exactly fifty years later, they and their children, grandchildren, surviving siblings, and in-laws gathered to celebrate their golden anniversary on a dinner cruise along the Potomac River. My siblings and I considered every detail except for who would photograph the festivities—a cardinal sin since my father had long ago worked part-time as a wedding photographer and had superbly chronicled our childhoods with his camera (see figure 7.4). On the anniversary cruise, we might have returned the favor. Instead, the camcorder was passed to my twelve-year-old nephew, who unintentionally produced a recording that was largely shaky, blurry, and poorly framed. However, his play-by-play commentary, which was intentionally over the top and hilarious, might have hinted that he could become a satirical talk show host or what he actually became—a lawyer. Ultimately, the video captured everyone in attendance, along with the river, the scenery, and a passenger plane gliding along the Potomac flight path to the recently renamed Washington Reagan National Airport. Precisely 367 days later, another plane departing from nearby Dulles International Airport and barreling toward the river was reported by air traffic control at Reagan National to be unresponsive. It crashed, intentionally, into the Pentagon.

Two years after the anniversary cruise, my mother had the first of the series of strokes that ultimately resulted in her placement in a nursing home, where she still lingers in a slow but steady decline. All four of my parents' siblings present for the cruise, starting with the youngest, my father's sister, are now gone, as is my father. Despite criticism that genealogy is a self-involved activity, recording or reviewing the births, marriages, and deaths in a family history can be a humbling exercise. It is impossible to escape the realization that no matter what you do, your life could eventually become distilled to a few basic facts.

The Maryland county near Washington, DC, where I grew up and where my mother, my brother, a sister, and a niece still live has experienced astonishing demographic changes. Whereas Italian, Irish, and Eastern European Americans along with other first- and second-generation immigrant families of European origins were once outsiders, Asian, Middle Eastern, and Latin American newcomers, among many others, now energize the area. DC's Chinatown has essentially migrated here across the District line, and an array of Asian and Latin American markets and *phở* restaurants dot the landscape. Narratives typical of "pre-chasm" genealogy that highlight diasporic struggles related to race and/or ethnicity emerge or will emerge no less from *these* families.

The collection of family members and branches that accumulated via social media and in-person encounters during my genealogical journey hint that the Global Family Reunion may be onto something in its efforts to link individual trees together to map the wider human family. When one recognizes that some of one's cousins—one's kin—speak different native languages and identify with what are considered racial minority cultures, it cannot help but raise awareness of the lives and rights of various groups.

In the wake of the 2016 US presidential election, many Americans and others around the world have plunged into a vortex of fear and uncertainty, and internal discord has erupted among many families, including the newly reconnected cousins on my family tree. At stake are many things, including one that *should* make America exceptional—diversity. Narratives can venture closer to capturing critical meaning in the lives of individuals and groups—diaries, letters, recorded reminiscences, interviews—and facilitate the making of connections with other histories and circumstances. Such narratives have been attached to many of the leaves on my family tree. For whatever it is worth, the story in these pages now serves as my own.

NOTES

CHAPTER 1: INTRODUCTION: GENEALOGY TODAY

1. Institutional Review Board (IRB) review of the ethnographic methodologies used in the investigation determined that they did not constitute human subject research. For the virtual ethnographic analysis of participatory cultures, the IRB at my institution has in the past considered such participants human subjects. However, there is recognition that those who post videos, blog essays, or similarly substantial material forgo assumptions of privacy when doing so. However, since respondents to such postings and other social media participants may have slightly higher expectations of anonymity, even though their posts can be searched, they are not cited by name or screen name. The virtual ethnography was considered strictly autobiographical—that is, it focused on the pivot points of thought and action that allowed *me* to interpret or react to a text or practice related to family history in a prescriptive manner that allowed development of the strategies illustrated in the volume.

CHAPTER 2: UNRAVELING GENEALOGY CULTURE

1. Harold Courlander, author of a 1967 novel, *The African*, sued Haley for plagiarism, winning a financial settlement and an admission by Haley that material from Courlander's book had made its way into *Roots*. Genealogists and historians have also questioned details in Haley's family history findings.

CHAPTER 5: TUBULAR GENEALOGY III: IDENTITY AND GENETIC ANCESTRY IN GENEALOGY TELEVISION AND RELATED TEXTS AND PRACTICES

1. The specific number of waves of migration, their means, timing, and locations, are still a matter of scientific dispute (see Lovgren).

CHAPTER 6: TUBULAR GENEALOGY IV: IDENTITY AND GENETIC ANCESTRY IN DIGITAL MEDIA AND RELATED TEXTS AND PRACTICES

1. Although this video has been removed, a YouTube search for the keywords *Italians white* brings up similar examples.

2. Unless otherwise noted, information from websites of testing providers is from 2013; details may subsequently have changed.

WORKS CITED

Alba, Richard, and Victor Nee. "Rethinking Assimilation Theory for a New Era of Immigration." *International Migration Review* 31.4 (1997): 826–74. Print.

Alexander, Bryan. "Affleck Tried to Hide His Slave-Owning 'Roots.'" *USA Today*, 19 April 2015. Web.

Ali, Nazia, and Andrew Holden. "Post-Colonial Pakistani Mobilities: The Embodiment of the 'Myth of Return' Tourism." *Mobilities* 1.2 (2006): 217–42. Print.

Amot, Chris. "Family History Boom Fuelled by Internet and TV." *The Guardian*, 5 July 2010. Web.

Anderson, Leon. "Analytic Autoethnography." *Journal of Contemporary Ethnography* 35.4 (2006): 373–95. Print.

Andrejevic, Mark. "Watching Television without Pity: The Productivity of Online Fans." *Television and New Media* 9.1 (2008): 24–46. Print.

Ansart, Séverine, Camille Pelat, Pierre-Yves Boelle, Fabrice Carrat, Antoine Flahault, and Alain-Jacques Vallerona. "Mortality Burden of the 1918–1919 Influenza Pandemic in Europe." *Influenza and Other Respiratory Viruses* 3 (2009): 99–106. Print.

Aprile, Pino. *Terroni: All That Has Been Done to Ensure That the Italians of the South Became "Southerners."* Trans. Ilaria Marra Rosiglioni. New York: Bordighera, 2011. Print.

Asiedu, Alex B. "Some Benefits of Migrants' Return Visits to Ghana." *Population, Space, and Place* 11 (2005): 1–11. Print.

Atkinson, Paul. "Rescuing Autoethnography." *Journal of Contemporary Ethnography* 35.4 (2006): 400–404. Print.

Aveling, Nado. "'Where Do You Come From?': Critical Storytelling as a Teaching Strategy within the Context of Teacher Education." *Discourse: Studies in the Cultural Politics of Education*, 22 (2001): 35–48. Print.

B, Anthony. "My Ancestry.com DNA Results!" Youtube.com, 18 July 2013. Web.

Basu, Paul. "Route Metaphors of 'Roots-Tourism' in the Scottish Highland Diaspora." In *Reframing Pilgrimage: Cultures in Motion*, ed. Simon Coleman and John Eade, 150–74. London: Routledge, 2004. Print.

Bell, Derrick, Jr. "Who's Afraid of Critical Race Theory?" *University of Illinois Law Review* 1995.4 (1995): 893–910. Print.

Benjamin, Walter. *Illuminations.* Trans. Harry Zohn. New York: Schocken, 1968. Print.

Bishop, Ronald. "'The Essential Force of the Clan': Developing a Collecting-Inspired Ideology of Genealogy through Textual Analysis." *Journal of Popular Culture* 38.6 (2005): 990–1010. Print.

Bishop, Ronald. "In the Grand Scheme of Things: An Exploration of the Meaning of Genealogical Research." *Journal of Popular Culture* 41.3 (2008): 393–412. Print.

Burns, Stanley. *Sleeping Beauty: Memorial Photography in America.* New York: Burns Archive, 2010. Print.

Carter, Sean. "Mobilizing *Hrvatsko*: Tourism and Politics in the Croatian Diaspora." In *Tourism, Diasporas, and Space,* ed. Tim Coles and Dallen J. Timothy, 188–201. New York: Routledge, 2004. Print.

Castells, Manuel. *The Internet Galaxy.* Oxford: Oxford University Press, 2001. Print.

Castells, Manuel. *The Rise of the Network Society.* 2nd ed. Oxford: Blackwell, 2000. Print.

Cepeda, Raquel. *Bird of Paradise: How I Became Latina.* New York: Atria, 2013. Kindle file.

"The Chasm." *Ancestry Insider,* 22 April 2013. Web.

Cole, Teju. "The White Savior Industrial Complex." *The Atlantic,* 21 March 2012. Web.

Collins, Patricia Hill. *Black Feminist Thought: Knowledge, Consciousness, and the Politics of Empowerment.* 2000; New York: Routledge Classics, 2009. Print.

Collins, Patricia Hill. "It's All in the Family: Intersections of Gender, Race, and Nation." *Hypatia* 13.3 (1998): 62–82. Print.

Commander Thsh. "REAL King Tut DNA Test = WHITE 100%." Youtube.com, 17 July 2013. Web.

Comunello, Francesca, ed. *Networked Sociability and Individualism: Technology for Personal and Professional Relationships.* Hershey, Penn.: IGI Global, 2012. Print.

Convey, Eric. "Women Sue 23andMe over Marketing Claims." *Bizjournals,* 19 December 2013. Web.

Cooke, Lisa L. "What Ancestry's Retirement of Family Tree Maker Software Means for You." *Lisa Louise Cooke's Genealogy Gems,* 8 December 2005. Web.

Cotton, Kim. "LGBT Genealogy." *Kim Cotton Research,* 20 October 2011. Web.

Courlander, Harold. *The African.* New York: Crown, 1967. Print.

Creet, Julia. *Need to Know: Ancestry and the Business of Family.* 2016. Film.

Crenshaw, Kimberlé Williams. "Beyond Racism and Misogyny: Black Feminism and 2 Live Crew." In *Words That Wound: Critical Race Theory, Assaultive Speech, and the First Amendment,* ed. Mari J. Matsuda, Charles R. Lawrence III, Richard Delgado, and Kimberlé Williams Crenshaw, 111–32. Boulder, Colo.: Westview, 1993. Print.

The Daily Show. Comedy Central. 20 July 2013. Television.

Dantò, Èzili. "'Avatar' Is a White Savior Movie." *The Progressive,* 5 January 2010. Web.

Davis, Jenny. "Networked: The New Social Operating System (A Review)." *Cyborgology,* 5 June 2012. Web.

Davis, Wendy. "Televisual Control: The Resistance of the Mockumentary." *Refractory: A Journal of Entertainment Media* 15.8 (2009). Web.

Del Boca, Lorenzo. *Polentoni: How and Why the North Was Betrayed.* Trans. Ilaria Marra Rosiglioni. New York: Bordighera, 2012. Print.

Dikomitis, Lisa. "A Moving Field: Greek Cypriot Refugees Returning 'Home.'" *Durham Anthropology Journal* 12.1 (2004): 7–20. Print.

DiStasi, Lawrence. "How World War II Iced Italian American Culture." In *Una Storia Segreta: The Secret History of Italian American Evacuation and Internment during World War II*, ed. Lawrence DiStasi, 303–12. Berkeley, Calif.: Heyday, 2001. Print.

Ellis, Carolyn, and Arthur Bochner. "Analyzing Analytic Autoethnography—An Autopsy." *Journal of Contemporary Ethnography* 35.4 (2006): 429–49. Print.

Erikson, Erik. *Childhood and Society*. 35th anniv. ed. New York: Norton, 1985. Print.

Everett, Chris S. "Melungeon History and Myth." *Appalachian Journal* 26.4 (1999): 358–409. Print.

Faris, Stephan. "In New Job, Italy's First Black Minister Confronts Culture of Casual Racism." *World Time*, 6 May 2013. Web.

Ferguson, Anthony W., and Warrick H. Chin. "A Treasury from the East: What We Can Learn from Chinese Genealogy." *Ensign*, October 1988. Web.

"Fewer Children May Explain Why More Women Now Outlive Men." *HealthDay*, 25 April 2016. Web.

Feyh, Kathleen. "On Carts and Horses: Post-Marxism in Pre-Post-Capitalism." *Journal of Communication Inquiry* 34.3 (2010): 234–40. Print.

Freeman, Mark. *Rewriting the Self: History, Memory, and Narrative*. London: Routledge, 1993. Print.

Gates, Henry L., Jr. "Ending the Slavery Blame Game." *New York Times*, 23 April 2010, A27. Print.

Gerbner, George, and Larry Gross. "Living with Television: The Violence Profile." *Journal of Communication* 26 (1972): 172–99. Print.

Giaccardi, Elisa, ed. *Heritage and Social Media: Understanding Heritage in a Participatory Culture*. New York: Routledge, 2012. Kindle file.

Goodstein, Laurie. "Mormons' Ad Campaign May Play Out on the '12 Campaign Trail." *New York Times*, 17 November 2011, A1. Web.

Greco, Lachrista. "Italian Americans and 'Whiteness.'" lachristogreco.com, 19 May 2011. Web.

Greely, Henry T. "Genetic Genealogy: Genetics Meets the Marketplace." In *Revisiting Race in a Genomic Age*, ed. Barbara A. Koenig, Sandra Soo-Jin Lee, and Sarah S. Richardson, 215–34. New Brunswick, N.J.: Rutgers University Press, 2008. Print.

Guelke, Jean Kay, and Dallen J. Timothy. "Locating Personal Pasts: An Introduction." In *Geography and Genealogy: Locating Personal Pasts*, ed. Dallen J. Timothy and Jeanne Kay Guelke, 1–20. Burlington, Vt.: Ashgate, 2008. Print.

Guglielmo, Jennifer, and Salvatore Salerno. *Are Italians White? How Race Is Made in America*. New York: Routledge, 2003. Print.

Haley, Alex. *Roots: The Saga of an American Family*. New York: Doubleday, 1976. Print.

Hall, Elaine J., and Marnie Salupo Rodriguez. "The Myth of Postfeminism." *Gender and Society* 17.6 (2003): 878–902. Print.

Hall, Stuart. "Cultural Identity and Diaspora." In *Identity, Community, Culture, Difference*, ed. Jonathan Rutherford, 222–37. London: Lawrence and Wishart, 1990. Print.

Hall, Stuart. "Encoding/Decoding." In *Culture, Media, Language*, ed. Stuart Hall, Dorothy Hobson, Andrew Lowe, and Paul Willis, 128–39. London: Hutchinson, 1980. Print.

Hall, Stuart. "The Whites of Their Eyes: Racist Ideologies and the Media." In *Gender, Race, and Class in Media*, 3rd ed., ed. Gail Dines and Jean M. Humez, 81–84. Thousand Oaks, Calif.: Sage, 2011. Print.

Hannam, Kevin. "India and the Ambivalences of Diaspora Tourism." In *Tourism, Diasporas, and Space*, ed. Tim Coles and Dallen J. Timothy, 246–60. New York: Routledge, 2004. Print.

Hasinoff, Amy Adele. "Contradictions of Participation: Critical Feminist Interventions in New Media Studies." *Communication and Critical/Cultural Studies* 11.3 (2014): 270–73. Print.

Hicks, Sherlynn. "A Reader Responds to TWOP/Bravo Deal: Freedom of Snark in Trouble?" *Adweek*, 15 March 2007. Web.

Hine, Christine. *Virtual Ethnography*. Thousand Oaks, Calif.: Sage, 2000. Print.

Hjorth, Larissa. "Locating the Visual: A Case Study of Gendered Location-Based Services and Camera Phone Practices in Seoul, South Korea." *Television and New Media* 15.1 (2014): 30–42. Print.

Horst, Heather A. "A Pilgrimage Home: Tombs, Burial, and Belonging in Jamaica." *Journal of Material Culture* 9.1 (2004): 111–26. Print.

"Immigration from Naples." *New York Times*, 5 August 1893, 4. Print.

"International Biosciences' Ancestry DNA Testing Results Feature in O'Dowd's Family Tree." www.ibdna.com, June 2013. Web.

ItalianBrownSkin. "Italians White? Since When?" Youtube.com, 18 October 2011. Web.

Jackson, John L. *Real Black: Adventures in Racial Sincerity*. Chicago: University of Chicago Press, 2005. Print.

Jacobson, Cardell, Phillip Kunz, and Melanie Conlin. "Extended Family Ties: Genealogical Researchers." In *Aging and the Family*, ed. Stephen Bahr and Evan Peterson, 193–205. Washington, DC: Lexington Books, 1989. Print.

Johnston, Druana. "Got My DNA Results from Ancestry.com, Part 1." Youtube.com, 21 January 2014. Web.

Jones, Jonathan. "Why Didn't People Smile in Old Photos?" *Guardian*, 12 August 2015. Web.

Joseph, Ralina L. "'Tyra Banks Is Fat': Reading (Post-)Racism and (Post-)Feminism in the New Millennium." In *Gender, Race, and Class in Media*, 3rd ed., ed. Gail Dines and Jean M. Humez, 519–29. Thousand Oaks, Calif.: Sage, 2011. Print.

Kayne, Eric. "Census: White Majority in U.S. Gone by 2043." *NBC News*, 13 June 2013. Web.

Kellner, Douglas. "Cultural Studies, Multiculturalism, and Media Culture." In *Gender, Race, and Class in Media*, 4th ed., ed. Gail Dines and Jean M. Humez, 7–19. Thousand Oaks, Calif.: Sage, 2015. Print.

Kelly, Mary E. "Ethnic Pilgrimages: People of Lithuanian Descent in Lithuania." *Sociological Spectrum* 20.1 (2000): 65–91. Print.

Kennett, Debbie. *DNA and Social Networking: A Guide to Genealogy in the Twenty-First Century.* Gloucestershire: History Press, 2012. Kindle file.

Khazan, Olga. "How Iceland's Genealogy Obsession Leads to Scientific Breakthroughs." *The Atlantic*, 7 October 2014. Web.

Koenig, Barbara, Sandra Soo-Jin Lee, and Sarah S. Richardson. "Introduction: Race and Genetics in a Genomic Age." In *Revisiting Race in a Genomic Age*, ed. Barbara A. Koenig. Sandra Soo-Jin Lee, and Sarah S. Richardson, 1–17. New Brunswick, N.J.: Rutgers University Press, 2008. Print.

Kozinets, Robert V. *Netnography: Doing Ethnographic Research Online.* Thousand Oaks, Calif.: Sage, 2009. Print.

Kramer, Anne-Marie. "Kinship, Affinity and Connectedness: Exploring the Role of Genealogy in Personal Lives." *Sociology* 45.3 (2011): 379–95. Print.

Kramer, Anne-Marie. "Mediatizing Memory: History, Affect, and Identity in *Who Do You Think You Are?*" *European Journal of Cultural Studies* 14.4 (2011): 428–45. Print.

Kuhn, Annette. *Family Secrets: Acts of Memory and Imagination.* 1995. London: Verso, 2002. Print.

Labrador, Angela M., and Elizabeth S. Chilton. "Re-Locating Meaning in Heritage Archives: A Call for Participatory Heritage Databases." *Proceedings of Computer Applications to Archaeology 2009.* Web.

Lambert, Ronald D. "The Family Historian and Temporal Orientations towards the Ancestral Past." *Time and Society* 5.2 (1996): 115–43. Print.

Lee, Catherine. "The Unspoken Significance of Gender in Constructing Kinship, Race, and Nation." In *Genetics and the Unsettled Past: The Collision of DNA, Race, and History*, ed. Keith Wailoo, Alondra Nelson, and Catherine Lee. New Brunswick, N.J.: Rutgers University Press, 2012. Kindle file.

Lee, Josephine. *The Japan of Pure Invention: Gilbert and Sullivan's The Mikado.* Minneapolis: University of Minnesota Press, 2010. Print.

Leonhardt, David. "Hispanics, the New Italians." *New York Times Sunday Review*, 20 April 2013, SR5. Print.

Levenson, Michael. "Mormons Baptized Slain Reporter Daniel Pearl." *Boston Globe*, 29 February 2012. Web.

Lew, Alan A., and Alan Wong. "Sojourners, *Guanxi*, and Clan Associations: Social Capital and Overseas Chinese Tourism to China." In *Tourism, Diasporas, and Space*, ed. Tim Coles and Dallen J. Timothy, 202–14. New York: Routledge, 2004. Print.

Lin, N. Kathy. "Orientalism and *The Mikado*: A Masterpiece Sits in the Shadow of Context." *Harvard Crimson*, 4 December 2007. Web.

Lindlof, Thomas R., and Bryan C. Taylor. *Qualitative Communication Research Methods.* 3rd ed. Thousand Oaks, Calif.: Sage, 2010. Print.

Live with Kelly and Michael. Syndicated. 2 September 2013. Television.

LLL Creations. Genealogy Word Art Designer Pack. 2014. Software.

Lovgren, Stefan. "Who Were the First Americans?" *National Geographic,* 3 September 2003. Web.

Lowry, Annie. "Income Gap, Meet the Longevity Gap." *New York Times,* 15 March 2014. Web.

Lozado, Carlos. "Who Is Latino?" *Washington Post,* 21 June 2013. Web.

MacEntee, Thomas. "Hiding Out in the Open: Researching LGBT Ancestors." *GeneaBloggers,* 10 October 2014. Web.

MacEntee, Thomas. "Is There a Perceived Age Demographic in Genealogy?" *High Definition Genealogy,* 29 August 2010. Web.

Madison, Kelly J. "Legitimation Crisis and Containment: The 'Anti-Racist White Hero' Film." *Critical Studies in Media Communication* 16.4 (1999): 399–416. Print.

Mangione, Jerre, and Ben Morreale. *La Storia: Five Centuries of the Italian American Experience.* New York: Harper Perennial, 1992. Print.

Maritz Research. "Sixty Percent of Americans Intrigued by Their Family Roots." 16 May 2000. Web.

McMillan, Douglas. "Family Trees 2.0." *Business Week,* 18 June 2007. Web.

Meethan, Kevin. "Remaking Time and Space: The Internet, Digital Archives, and Genealogy." In *Geography and Genealogy: Locating Personal Pasts,* ed. Dallen J. Timothy and Jeanne Kay Guelke, 99–114. Burlington, Vt.: Ashgate, 2008. Print.

The Melissa Harris Perry Show. MSNBC. 31 May 2015. Television.

Miconi, Andrea. "Lee Rainie and Barry Wellman, *Networked: The New Social Operating System.*" *International Journal of Communication* 7 (2013): 954–59. Print.

Miller, Gerri. "'Faces of America' Reveals Eva Longoria Parker's Surprising Roots." *Latina,* 2 February 2010. Web.

Miller, Lisa. "Skip Gates' Next Big Idea." *Newsweek,* 18 April 2011, 42–45. Print.

Moe, Nelson. *The View from Vesuvius: Italian Culture and the Southern Question.* Berkeley: University of California Press, 2006. Kindle file.

Mook, Ben. "PBS, NPR Reps Discuss Challenges of Reaching New Audiences with SXSW Attendees." *Current,* 17 March 2015. Web.

Mountain, David C., and Jeanne K. Guelke. "Genetics, Genealogy, and Geography." In *Geography and Genealogy: Locating Personal Pasts,* ed. Dallen J. Timothy and Jeanne Kay Guelke, 153–74. Burlington, Vt.: Ashgate, 2008. Print.

Murji, Karim, and John Solomos. "Introduction: Racialization in Theory and Practice." In *Racialization: Studies in Theory and Practice,* ed. Karim Murji and John Solomos, 1–27. New York: Oxford University Press, 2005. Print.

Nakamura, Lisa. "'Where Do You Want to Go Today?': Cybernetic Tourism, the Internet, and Transnationality." In *Race in Cyberspace,* ed. Beth E. Kolko, Lisa Nakamura, and Gilbert B. Rodman, 15–26. New York. Routledge, 2000. Print.

Nash, Catherine. "Genealogical Identities." *Environment and Planning D: Society and Space* 20 (2002): 27–52. Print.

Nash, Catherine. "Genetic Kinship." *Cultural Studies* 18.1 (2004): 1–33. Print.

Nash, Catherine. "Mapping Origins: Race and Relatedness in Population Genetics and Genetic Genealogy." In *New Genetics, New Identities*, ed. Paul Atkinson, Peter Glasner, and Helen Greenslade, 77–100. New York: Routledge. 2007. Print.

Nelson, Alondra. "Bio Science: Genetic Genealogy Testing and the Pursuit of African Ancestry." *Social Studies of Science* 38.5 (2008): 759–83. Print.

Nelson, Alondra, and Won Hwang. "Roots and Revelation: Genetic Ancestry Testing and the YouTube Generation." In *Race after the Internet*, ed. Lisa Nakamura and Peter A. Chow-White, 271–90. New York: Routledge, 2012. Print.

Nguyen, Thu Huong, and Brian King. "The Culture of Tourism in the Diaspora: The Case of the Vietnamese Community in Australia." In *Tourism, Diasporas, and Space*, ed. Tim Coles and Dallen J. Timothy, 172–87. New York: Routledge, 2004. Print.

Omi, Michael, and Howard Winant. *Racial Formation in the United States: From the 1960s to the 1990s.* 2nd ed. New York: Routledge, 1994. Print.

L'Oltreuomo. "Le Mappe degli Stereotipi Europei." 4 October 2013. Web.

Ono, Kent. A. "Postracism: A Theory of the 'Post-' as Political Strategy." *Journal of Communication Inquiry* 34.3 (2010): 227–33. Print.

Otterstrom, Samuel M. "Genealogy as Religious Ritual: The Doctrine and Practice of Family History in the Church of Jesus Christ of Latter-day Saints." In *Geography and Genealogy: Locating Personal Pasts*, ed. Dallen J. Timothy and Jeanne Kay Guelke, 137–51. Burlington, Vt.: Ashgate, 2008. Print.

Overmire, Laurence. *One Immigrant's Legacy: The Overmyer Family in America, 1751–2009: A Biographical Record of Revolutionary War Veteran Capt. John George Overmire and His Descendants.* West Lynn, Ore.: Indelible Mark, 2009. Print.

Pappas, Stephanie. "King Tut Related to Half of European Men? Maybe Not." *LiveScience*, 3 August 2011. Web.

Passel, Jeffrey S. "Census History: Counting Hispanics." *Pew Research Center*, 3 March 2010. Web.

Perrone, Matthew. "23andMe Faces Class Action Lawsuit in California." *NBC News*, 3 December 2013. Web.

Podolsky, Jeffrey. "Henry Louis Gates Premieres 'Faces of America,' Finds Out He's Related to Regis Philbin." *Speakeasy: Wall Street Journal Blogs*, 2 February 2010. Web.

Pollack, Andrew. "23andMe Will Resume Giving Users Health Data." *New York Times*, 21 October 2015. Web.

Powell, Kimberly. "How to Handle Adoption in the Family Tree: Do I Trace My Adopted Family, Birth Family, or Both?" Genealogy.about.com, 25 December 2014. Web.

"Race and Science." *PBS*, 2006. Web.

Rainie, Lee, and Barry Wellman. *Networked: The New Social Operating System*. Cambridge: MIT Press, 2012. Kindle File.

"RootsTech Attendee Demographics." *Ancestry Insider*, 29 June 2015. Web.

Saar, Martin. "Genealogy and Subjectivity." *European Journal of Philosophy* 10.2 (2002): 231–45. Print.

Said, Edward. *Orientalism*. New York: Vintage, 1978. Print.

Sanchez, George J. "Face the Nation: Race, Immigration, and the Rise of Nativism in Late Twentieth Century America." *International Migration Review* 34.3 (1997): 826–74. Print.

Sarahize, Khalif. "REAL King Tut DNA Test = BLACK 100%." Youtube.com, 4 December 2012. Web.

Saturday Night Live. NBC. 8 April 2017. Television.

Schramm, Katharina. "Genomics on Route: Ancestry, Heritage, and the Politics of Identity across the Black Atlantic." In *Identity Politics and the New Genetics: Re/Creating Categories of Difference and Belonging*, ed. Katharina Schramm, David Skinner, and Richard Rottenburg, 167–92. New York: Berghahn, 2012. Print.

Scodari, Christine. "'No Politics Here': Age and Gender in Soap Opera 'Cyberfandom.'" *Women's Studies in Communication* 21.2 (1998): 168–87. Print.

Scodari, Christine. *Serial Monogamy: Soap Opera, Lifespan, and the Gendered Politics of Fantasy*. Cresskill, N.J.: Hampton, 2004. Print..

Shanks, Pete. "Genomic Controversy in Iceland: Déja Vu All Over Again." *Biopolitical Times*, 28 May 2014. Web.

Shute, Nancy. "New Routes to Old Roots." *Smithsonian*, March 2002, 76–81. Print.

Silberman, Neil, and Margaret Purser. "Collective Memory as Affirmation: People-Centered Cultural Heritage in a Digital Age." In *Heritage and Social Media: Understanding Heritage in a Participatory Culture*, ed. Elisa Giaccardi. New York: Routledge, 2012. Kindle file.

Silman, Anna. "From the Duggars to Honey Boo Boo: How TLC Became the Most Controversial Channel on Television." *Salon*, 27 May 2015. Web.

Sleeter, Christine. "Critical Family History, Identity, and Historical Memory." *Educational Studies* 4.2 (2008): 114–24. Print.

Smart, Andrew, Richard Tutton, Paul Martin, and George T. H. Ellison. "'Race' as a Social Construction in Genetics." In *Identity Politics and the New Genetics: Re/Creating Categories of Difference and Belonging*, ed. Katharina Schramm, David Skinner, and Richard Rottenburg, 30–52. New York: Berghahn, 2012. Print.

Spickard, Paul. *Almost All Aliens: Immigration, Race, and Colonialism in American History and Identity*. New York: Routledge, 2007. Print.

Springer, Kimberly. "Divas, Evil Black Bitches, and Bitter Black Women: African-American Women in Postfeminist and Post–Civil-Rights Popular Culture." In *Interrogating Post-Feminism: Gender and the Politics of Popular Culture*, ed. Yvonne Tasker and Diane Negra, 249–76. Durham, NC: Duke University Press. 2007. Print.

Squires, Catherine R. "Running through the Trenches; or, An Introduction to the Undead Culture Wars and Dead Serious Identity Politics." *Journal of Communication Inquiry* 34.3 (2010): 210–14. Print.

Statue of Liberty–Ellis Island Foundation. https://www.libertyellisfoundation.org/. Web.

Stone, Andrea. "Elie Wiesel: Mitt Romney Should Tell Mormon Church to Stop Performing Posthumous Proxy Baptisms on Jews." *Huffington Post*, 14 February 2012. Web.

Sykes, Brian. *The Seven Daughters of Eve: The Science That Reveals Our Genetic Ancestry.* New York: Norton, 2001. Print.

Tabatabaie, Vafa, Gil Atzmon, Swapnil N. Rajpathak, Ruth Freeman, Nir Barzilai, and Jill Crandall. "Exceptional Longevity Is Associated with Decreased Reproduction." *Aging* 3.12 (2011): 1202–5. Print.

Tanner, James. "The Genealogy Age Gap—How Do We Expand to Include the Youth?" *Genealogy's Star*, 9 March 2013. Web.

Tasker, Yvonne, and Diane Negra. "Introduction: Feminist Politics and Postfeminist Culture." In *Interrogating Post-Feminism: Gender and the Politics of Popular Culture*, ed. Yvonne Tasker and Diane Negra, 1–25. Durham, NC: Duke University Press, 2007. Print.

Television without Pity. Televisionwithoutpity.com. Web. Defunct; archived at http://www.brilliantbutcancelled.com/shows/.

Timothy, Dallen J. "Genealogical Mobility: Tourism and the Search for a Personal Past." In *Geography and Genealogy: Locating Personal Pasts*, ed. Dallen J. Timothy and Jeanne Kay Guelke, 115–35. Burlington, Vt.: Ashgate, 2008. Print.

Tsvetkov, Yanko. *Atlas of Prejudice: The Complete Stereotype Map Collection.* 2nd ed. N.p.: Alphadesigner, 2017. Print.

Tuchman, Gaye. *Hearth and Home: Images of Women in the Mass Media.* New York: Oxford University Press, 1978. Print.

TV Guide (UK). tvguide.co.uk. Web.

Tyler, Katharine. "The Genealogical Imagination: The Inheritance of Interracial Identities." *Sociological Review* 53.3 (2005): 476–94. Print.

Umfleet, S. Brady. "Genealogy and Generativity in Older Adults." Master's project, San Jose State University, 2009. Print.

Valdivia, Angharad. "The Gendered Face of Latinidad: Global Circulation of Hybridity." In *Circuits of Visibility: Gender and Transnational Cultures*, ed. Radha Sarma Hegde. New York: New York University Press, 2011. Kindle file.

Wachtel, Nathan. "Memory and History: Introduction." *History and Anthropology* 12.2 (1986): 207–24. Print.

Wade, Peter. "Race, Kinship, and the Ambivalence of Identity." In *Identity Politics and the New Genetics: Re/Creating Categories of Difference and Belonging*, ed. Katharina Schramm, David Skinner, and Richard Rottenburg, 79–96. New York: Berghahn, 2012. Print.

Wailoo, Keith. "Who Am I?: Genes and the Problem of Historical Identity." In *Genetics and the Unsettled Past: The Collision of DNA, Race, and History*, ed. Keith Wailoo, Alondra Nelson, and Catherine Lee. New Brunswick, N.J.: Rutgers University Press, 2012. Kindle file.

Watts, Eric King. "The (Nearly) Apocalyptic Politics of 'Postracial' America; or, 'This Is Now the United States of Zombieland.'" *Journal of Communication Inquiry* 34.3 (2010): 214–22. Print.

Wee, Eric. "A Forest of Family Trees." *Washington Post*, 4 July 1997, A1. Print.

Weil, François. *Family Trees: A History of Genealogy in America*. Cambridge: Harvard University Press, 2013. Kindle file.

Weldon, Victoria. "Revealed: Scandal of Scotland's Rich-Poor Life Expectancy Divide for Women." *HeraldScotland*, 5 March 2016. Web.

Wellman, Barry. "Little Boxes, Glocalization, and Networked Individualism." In *Digital Cities II: Computational and Sociological Approaches*, ed. Makoto Tanabe, Peter van den Besselaar, and Toru Ishida, 10–25. Berlin: Springer. 2002. Print.

Wells, Spencer. *The Journey of Man: A Genetic Odyssey*. Princeton: Princeton University Press, 2002. Print.

Whittington, Mark. "Niall of the Nine Hostages Is Ancestor of Gates and Crowley." Yahoo, 29 July 2009. Web.

Williams, Raymond. *Marxism and Literature*. Oxford: Oxford University Press, 1977. Print.

Woods, Corinne. "The Great Debate: How Technology Widens the Gender Gap." Reuters, 21 March 2014. Web.

Young, James E. *The Texture of Memory: Holocaust Memorials and Meaning*. New Haven: Yale University Press, 1993. Print.

Zelizer, Barbie. "Reading the Past against the Grain: The Shape of Memory Studies." *Critical Studies in Mass Communication* 12.2 (1995): 214–39. Print.

Zimmer, Carl. "Charlemagne's DNA and Our Universal Royalty." *National Geographic*, 7 May 2003. Web.

INDEX

CPSIA information can be obtained
at www.ICGtesting.com
Printed in the USA
BVHW04*1052220518
516606BV00005B/7/P